Exploring iPad®

FOR DUMMIES®

2nd Edition

by Galen Gruman

Published by
John Wiley & Sons, Inc.
111 River Street
Hoboken, NJ 07030-5774
www.wiley.com

Copyright © 2012 by John Wiley & Sons, Inc.,
Hoboken, New Jersey

Published by John Wiley & Sons, Inc.,
Hoboken, New Jersey

Published simultaneously in Canada

Trademarks: Wiley, the Wiley logo, For
Dummies, the Dummies Man logo, A
Reference for the Rest of Us!, The Dummies
Way, Dummies Daily, The Fun and Easy
Way, Dummies.com, Making Everything
Easier, and related trade dress are trademarks
or registered trademarks of John Wiley &
Sons, Inc. and/or its affiliates in the United
States and other countries, and may not be
used without written permission. iPad is
a registered trademark of Apple, Inc. All
other trademarks are the property of their
respective owners. John Wiley & Sons, Inc.,
is not associated with any product or vendor
mentioned in this book.

LIMIT OF LIABILITY/DISCLAIMER OF
WARRANTY: THE PUBLISHER AND THE
AUTHOR MAKE NO REPRESENTATIONS
OR WARRANTIES WITH RESPECT TO THE
ACCURACY OR COMPLETENESS OF THE
CONTENTS OF THIS WORK AND SPECIFICALLY
DISCLAIM ALL WARRANTIES, INCLUDING
WITHOUT LIMITATION WARRANTIES OF
FITNESS FOR A PARTICULAR PURPOSE.
NO WARRANTY MAY BE CREATED OR
EXTENDED BY SALES OR PROMOTIONAL
MATERIALS. THE ADVICE AND STRATEGIES
CONTAINED HEREIN MAY NOT BE SUITABLE
FOR EVERY SITUATION. THIS WORK IS
SOLD WITH THE UNDERSTANDING THAT
THE PUBLISHER IS NOT ENGAGED IN
RENDERING LEGAL, ACCOUNTING, OR OTHER
PROFESSIONAL SERVICES. IF PROFESSIONAL
ASSISTANCE IS REQUIRED, THE SERVICES
OF A COMPETENT PROFESSIONAL PERSON
SHOULD BE SOUGHT. NEITHER THE
PUBLISHER NOR THE AUTHOR SHALL BE
LIABLE FOR DAMAGES ARISING HEREFROM.
THE FACT THAT AN ORGANIZATION OR
WEBSITE IS REFERRED TO IN THIS WORK
AS A CITATION AND/OR A POTENTIAL
SOURCE OF FURTHER INFORMATION DOES
NOT MEAN THAT THE AUTHOR OR THE
PUBLISHER ENDORSES THE INFORMATION
THE ORGANIZATION OR WEBSITE MAY
PROVIDE OR RECOMMENDATIONS IT MAY
MAKE. FURTHER, READERS SHOULD BE
AWARE THAT INTERNET WEBSITES LISTED
IN THIS WORK MAY HAVE CHANGED OR
DISAPPEARED BETWEEN WHEN THIS WORK
WAS WRITTEN AND WHEN IT IS READ.

For general information on our other
products and services, please contact our
Customer Care Department within the U.S.
at 877-762-2974, outside the U.S. at 317-572-
3993, or fax 317-572-4002.

For technical support, please visit www.
wiley.com/techsupport.

Wiley also publishes its books in a variety of
electronic formats. Some content that appears
in print may not be available in electronic
books.

ISBN: 978-1-118-39863-0

Manufactured in the United States of America
10 9 8 7 6 5 4 3 2 1

Contents

Publisher's Acknowledgments

We're proud of this book; please send us your comments through our online registration form located at http://dummies.custhelp.com. For other comments, please contact our Customer Care Department within the U.S. at 877-762-2974, outside the U.S. at 317-572-3993, or fax 317-572-4002.

Some of the people who helped bring this bookazine to market include the following:

Acquisitions and Editorial

Project Editor: Kim Darosett

Acquisitions Editor: Kyle Looper

Copy Editors: Virginia Sanders, Heidi Unger

Editorial Manager: Leah Michael

Sr. Editorial Assistant: Cherie Case

Composition Services

Project Coordinator: Kristie Rees

Layout and Graphics: Kathie Rickard

Proofreader: Rebecca Denoncour, John Greenough

Text Compiler: Carol Person

Publishing and Editorial for Technology Dummies

Richard Swadley, Vice President and Executive Group Publisher

Andy Cummings, Vice President and Publisher

Mary Bednarek, Executive Acquisitions Director

Mary C. Corder, Editorial Director

Publishing for Consumer Dummies

Kathleen Nebenhaus, Vice President and Executive Publisher

Composition Services

Debbie Stailey, Director of Composition Services

Front cover (top): © franckreporter/iStockphoto.com

Back cover: © Troels Graugaard/iStockphoto.com

DUMMIES

Introduction

*Y*ou have to wonder if anyone ever sleeps at Apple. Every year since 2010, there's been a new iPad model, and every year since 2007, there's been a new version of iOS, the operating system that powers the iPad, iPhone, and iPod touch. That's meant a big change for iPad users every six months: either a new model or a revamped iOS. The latest big change is the third-generation iPad, popularly called the iPad 3 and iPad HD. It adds a better screen, better graphics, faster cellular connections, and dictation capabilities. And it has all the innovations of 2011's iOS 5 and the free iCloud syncing service. The combination of the new iPad, iOS 5, and iCloud is simply amazing for fun, business, and just staying in touch. My goal is to deliver the key information on iOS 5, iCloud, and the iPad itself in a light and breezy fashion. I expect you to have fun using your iPad. I equally hope that you have fun spending time with me.

> *...amazing for* ***fun, business,*** *and just* ***staying*** *in touch***

As with most Apple products, the iPad is beautifully designed and intuitive to use. And though my editors may not want me to reveal this dirty little secret (especially on the first page, for goodness sake), the truth is you'll get pretty far just by exploring the iPad's many functions and features on your own, without the help of this (or any other) documentation. Okay, now that I spilled the beans, I'll tell you why you shouldn't run back to the store and request a refund. This publication is chock-full of useful tips, advice, and other nuggets that should make your iPad experience all the more pleasurable for both versions of the iPad. I'd even go as far as to say you won't find some of these nuggets anywhere else. So keep this bookazine nearby and consult it often — but most important, enjoy your iPad!

Meet the iPad!

● *What you get with an iPad* ● *The iPad's controls* ● *Setting up and managing the iPad*

You've read about the iPad. You've seen news coverage of the lines at Apple Stores on the day it was released. You're so intrigued that you've decided to get your own iPad to have fun, explore the online world, read e-books, organize your photos, and more.

You've made a good decision because the iPad redefines the computing experience in an exciting new way. It's also an absolutely perfect fit for so many people: students, families, seniors, and business-people. Why? Because you can do so much with it, from accessing the web to reading books to playing games.

The newest model brings an amazingly sharp, detailed screen called the Retina display that transforms text and has opened the door to eye-popping games, HD movie-watching, and pro-level photo editing. And that's on top of the third-gen iPad's inherited ability to change the screen display as you rotate the tablet, adjust the screen brightness to the surrounding light, and let you use your fingers to do so many activities.

iPad Models and Pricing

Model	Storage	Wi-Fi	Wi-Fi/Cellular
iPad 2	16GB	$399/£329	3G $529/£429
Third-Gen	16GB	$499/£399	4G $629/£499
Third-Gen	32GB	$599/£479	4G $729/£579
Third-Gen	64GB	$699/£559	4G $829/£659

iPad on the Front
Status bar
Camera (except original iPad)
Application icons
Multi-Touch display
Home button

Photo by Ingall W. Bull III

DUMMIES

The iPad Controls

The iPad has many best-of-class features, but perhaps its most unusual feature is the lack of a physical keyboard or stylus. Instead, it has a 9.7-inch, super-high-resolution touchscreen (264 pixels per inch on the third-gen iPad and 132 pixels per inch on the iPad 2, if you care about such things) that you operate by using a pointing device you're already intimately familiar with: your finger.

iPad on the Front

- **The (all-important) Home button:** On the iPad, you go back to the Home screen to do just about anything. If you're browsing online and you want to open the calendar, push the Home button to switch from the web browser to the Home screen, where you find the Calendar app. No matter where you are, push Home and you're back to home base.

- **The Multi-Touch display:** And what a display it is! You've never seen a more beautiful screen on a handheld device in your life.

- **The camera (except the original iPad):** For FaceTime videoconferencing or snapping your own picture, the rear camera is a nice convenience.

iPad on the Top

- **Sleep/Wake button:** You can use this button to power up your iPad, put it in sleep mode, wake it up, or power it down.

- **Headphone jack and microphone:** If you want to listen to your music in private, you can plug in a 3.5mm minijack headphone (including an iPhone headset [if you have one], which gives you bidirectional sound). There's also a tiny microphone that makes it possible to speak into your iPad to do things like make phone calls using Internet calling services.

iPad on the Bottom

- **Dock connector slot:** This is where you plug in the dock connector cord to charge your battery or sync with your Mac OS or Windows computer.

- **(A tiny, mighty) speaker:** One of the iPad's nice surprises is what a great little sound system it has and how much sound this tiny speaker produces. It is located on the bottom edge of the iPad.

iPad on the Side

- **Side switch:** It's configurable, and you can set it to disable screen rotation or alerts sounds, such as those for new messages, so they don't interrupt your music or video program.

- **Volume:** A volume rocker you tap up for more volume and down for less.

Older computers, most iPod and iPhone charging blocks, and most USB hubs don't have enough power to charge the iPad, in which case the iPad displays "Not charging" in the status bar. If you see this message, use the 10W charging block that came with the iPad.

Nice-to-have iPad add-ons

Apple's iPad Case is arguably the best case to protect your iPad 1, and the Apple Smart Cover is likewise arguably the best cover to protect your third-gen iPad's or iPad 2's screen. The material is easy to keep clean and is easy to hold, but the best feature is its ability to act as a stand for the iPad, putting it in a perfect typing position. The only flaw of the iPad Case: It gets in the way of the dock connectors, even on Apple's docks. (The Smart Cover doesn't have this issue.)

The clear cylinder stands for the iPad at the Apple Store are unfortunately not for sale. But you might like the Loop from Griffin Technology, which is a cool-looking stand. It lets you hold your iPad at three different angles, and it holds your iPad even if the iPad is wrapped in the Apple iPad Case or has the Smart Cover attached.

Not everyone likes the standard Apple earbuds, which fit inside the earlobes. Fortunately, you can use any iPod earbud or earphone that you prefer. Be sure to get one with a microphone if you plan to use Skype or other voice applications.

The final essential add-on is a glass-cleaning cloth, such as what's used for camera lenses, to wipe away the fingerprints that accumulate on the Pad's screen. Just buff away the fingerprints to get a clean screen.

The iPad's screen rotates unless the screen rotation lock is engaged. So the iPad screen might be rotating back and forth as you move, depending on how you're holding the iPad while you're reading in bed or web-surfing while sitting on the couch. That's a good time to use the rotation lock. If the side switch isn't set for rotation lock, do so by double-pressing the Home button and swiping to the right to reveal the onscreen controls. Then tap the Rotation Lock icon.

Setup and registration

The first time you turn on your iPad, you have to register it, either to your existing iTunes account or, if you don't have one yet, to a newly created one. In iOS 5, you can do the setup from your computer via iTunes or directly over the Internet (if you have a Wi-Fi connection) via Apple's servers. Note that you need to have iTunes 10.5 on your Mac or PC to install iOS 5, and you need iTunes 10.6 to work with a third-gen iPad or any iPad running iOS 5.1.

From iTunes:

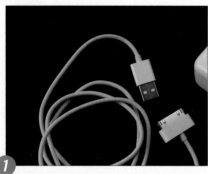

1 Connect the iPad to your computer's USB port using the cable that came with the iPad and turn it on by pressing the Home or the Sleep/Wake button. You see the famous Apple logo, followed a minute or so later by a screen with the default background.

2 In iTunes, you see a screen that lets you register your iPad; click Continue to do so. Fill in the required information, and when you're done, click Continue. Now your iPad is registered. But iTunes isn't finished.

3 In the Set Up Your iPad window, select any or all of the three Automatically Sync options to have those items sync automatically when you connect the iPad to your computer. Also give the iPad a name in the Name field. Click Continue when you're done.

Without iTunes:

1 Turn on the iPad. A splash screen with the word *iPad* appears; tap Continue.

TIP

If you bought a cellular model, you have one more setup step: registering your iPad with the carrier whose cellular data service you bought. Doing so is simple: Go to the Settings app and then tap the Cellular Data option in the Sidebar. In the Cellular Data pane that opens on the right, make sure the Cellular Data slider is set to On. (Drag it to On if not.) Then choose your desired data plan.

2 Go through the various setup screens, which ask about detecting your location, connecting to a Wi-Fi network, restoring from a backup (such as if you are upgrading from a previous model), signing up via your Apple ID (or creating a new Apple ID), using iCloud (and setting up a free iCloud account if needed), using the free Find My iPad service, and enabling diagnostic information to be sent to Apple.

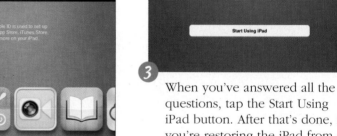

3 When you've answered all the questions, tap the Start Using iPad button. After that's done, if you're restoring the iPad from a backup, your apps, media files, and settings are then restored in a process than can take tens of minutes to complete.

DUMMIES

The iPad status bar

At the top of the iPad screen is the status bar, which displays various icons based on its current status.

Icon	Its Name	What It Does
	Battery Life	Shows you how much battery power is remaining; at left is a percentage
	Charging	Indicates that the iPad's battery is being charged
	Bluetooth	Displays when Bluetooth is turned on in the Settings app
	Rotation Lock	Displays in the status bar if you've turned on the rotation lock
	Wi-Fi	Shows up when your iPad is connected to the Internet over a Wi-Fi network. The more semicircular lines you see (up to three), the stronger the Wi-Fi signal is.
	Accessing	Indicates that data is being loaded into your iPad via Wi-Fi or cellular radio
	Airplane Mode	Turns off all wireless features of your iPad and makes it possible to enjoy music or video during your flight. Turn Airplane mode on or off in the Settings app.
	Location	Indicates that your current location is being tracked by the app you are using
	Syncing	Indicates that the iPad is syncing content or other information with your computer or iCloud
	Playback	Indicates that the iPad is playing audio, video, or other media content through its speakers, via an HDMI cable, or over AirPlay wireless streaming (the status bar turns blue when AirPlay is active)
VPN	VPN	Indicates that a secure virtual private network is active between your iPad and a (usually) corporate network

Wi-Fi/Cellular Models Only

Icon	Its Name	What It Does
LTE	4G LTE	Informs you that you are connected to your carrier's high-speed 4G LTE wireless network and can connect to the Internet
3G	3G	Informs you that you are connected to your carrier's mid-speed 3G wireless network and can connect to the Internet
E	EDGE	Tells you that your wireless carrier's lower-speed EDGE network (on AT&T and other GSM networks only) is available, and you can use it to connect to the Internet
o	2G	Says that your wireless carrier's low-speed 2G data network is available and that your iPad can use it to connect to the Internet
	Cellular Signal Strength	Tells you how strong the signal is for the current cellular connection (4G LTE, 3G, EDGE, or 2G): the more bars (up to five), the better

On and Off; Locked and Unlocked

To turn off the device completely, press and hold the Sleep/Wake button until a red arrow appears at the top of the screen. Then drag the arrow from the left to the right. Tap Cancel at the bottom of the screen if you change your mind.

To turn on the iPad, press either the Sleep/Wake button or the Home button — that's it!

You may not think it's necessary to lock an iPad when you're not using it; after all, it just goes to sleep at some point. But there are sound reasons for locking an iPad:

✔ You can't inadvertently turn it on.

✔ You keep prying eyes at bay.

✔ You spare the battery some juice.

Apple makes it a cinch to lock the iPad. In fact, you don't need to do anything to lock the iPad; it happens automatically as long as you don't touch the screen for a minute or two. (You can also set the amount of time it takes before the iPad automatically locks in the Settings app.) Can't wait? Just press the Sleep/Wake button.

Unlocking the iPad is easy, too. Here's how it works:

① Press the Sleep/Wake button. Or, press the Home button on the front of the screen. The on-screen slider appears.

② Drag the slider to the right with your finger.

③ In some cases, you also need to enter a passcode. For example, if you have set a passcode in the Settings app (tap General and then Passcode Lock to set your passcode).

Making the iPad Work Your Way

Although the iPad is amazingly simple to use, it has lots and lots of capabilities. To make adjustments, use the Settings app. The settings for the iPad itself and for Apple's built-in apps are at the top of the left pane; if any apps you installed have settings, they appear at the bottom of that pane.

The General pane — tap General in the left pane to see it — has most of the iPad controls, such as for sounds, locking, date and time, keyboard, Wi-Fi syncing, side switch settings, restrictions on what apps can run and what services (for example, in-app purchasing) are permitted, networking (Wi-Fi and, for corporate access, VPN), and Bluetooth connectivity. Use the iCloud pane (in iOS 5) to set up backup and syncing of media, e-mail, contacts, and more via Apple's iCloud service.

Two other Settings app controls are worth pointing out: Brightness & Wallpaper, for adjusting the screen display, and Picture Frame, for having your iPad work as an electronic photo frame when idle.

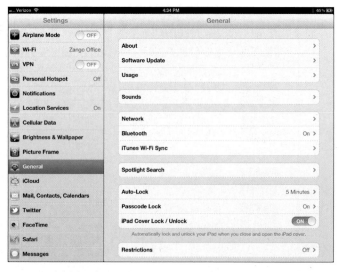

The Settings app is where you adjust many iPad settings.

DUMMIES

Getting Connected

IN THIS ARTICLE

- *Going online via Wi-Fi*
- *Using cellular networks to get connected*

Getting on the Internet with your iPad is easy using its Wi-Fi capabilities or, on the Wi-Fi/cellular models, its 3G or 4G capabilities. When you're online, the built-in browser, Safari, is your ticket to a wide world of information, entertainment, education, and more. If you've used a Mac, you already know how to use Safari, though the way you move around will be new to you on the touchscreen iPad. But if Safari is new to you, you'll find its basic elements are similar to those in any browser.

Internet-oriented apps such as e-mail and news readers also go online via Wi-Fi or cellular connections. The iPad automatically hops onto the fastest available network, which is almost always Wi-Fi. Wi-Fi comes in several variations (802.11a, b, g, and n), and the iPad supports them all, so don't worry about Wi-Fi versions.

Connecting via Wi-Fi

Wi-Fi is what you use to connect to a home network or your local coffee shop hotspot network. Wi-Fi has a reasonably limited range of typically 100 feet or so within buildings, so it's not something you can count on wherever you happen to be. Also, Wi-Fi access in many hotspots requires a subscription; a password may be required in other hotspots.

When you're in range of a hotspot, you may see a message asking you to select one of several nearby networks (or you may see only one). After you tap on one, enter the network's password and tap the Join button. You can disable this message in the iPad's Settings application.

Tap the Wi-Fi option from the list in the Sidebar. In the pane at right, move the Ask to Join Networks slider to Off.

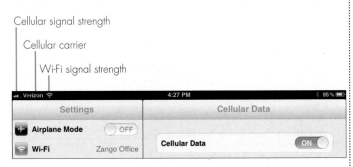

Cellular signal strength
Cellular carrier
Wi-Fi signal strength

Indicators for cellular and Wi-Fi appear in the status bar

Using 3G and 4G Networks

Wi-Fi is a great way to connect at a home or office because you usually pay a flat fee each month as part of your broadband service to use as much data as you want. And at cafés and hotels, it's long been a reliable way to get connected for a small fee. But over the last decade, cellular carriers have been building out their networks' data services that provide Internet connectivity from almost anywhere. The 3G networks available in most regions provide reasonable speeds — less than Wi-Fi but enough for most tasks — so Apple has always had iPad models that can use these services. A faster variant of such cellular networks, called 4G LTE, is now being rolled out globally, and the third-gen iPad can run on the 4G networks where available and on the 3G networks elsewhere.

Unlike the case for smartphones in the U.S. and Canada, you don't need a contract to use the iPad on a carrier's network. Instead, you pay for a specific amount of data; when you've used that data or after 30 days, you choose whether to buy another increment of data. That way, you can buy it just when you need it.

Even better, all iPad models — except the iPad 2's Verizon version — let you get a MicroSIM card in any country you visit so you can use a local carrier's network at local prices, which can be a hundredth the cost of international data roaming. MicroSIMs usually cost $10, £10, or €10. (A MicroSIM is what the carrier uses to authorize the connection of your device to its network and track your usage.) Outside the U.S., you can even change local carriers by getting a different provider's MicroSIM. (The Verizon iPad 2 lacks such a MicroSIM, so you can't use local services, but the third-gen Verizon iPad can.)

Use the Cellular Data pane in the Settings app to turn your cellular service on or off, enable or disable roaming, and enable or disable 4G (on a third-gen iPad). You can also set a lock on the MicroSIM that requires a password to get network access, to avoid losing your data allotment if your iPad is lost or stolen.

Sample Cellular Data Rates

Country	Carrier	Data Increment and Price
U.S.	AT&T	250MB: $15, 3GB: $30
	Verizon Wireless	1GB: $20, 2GB: $30
Canada	Bell	250MB: $15, 5GB: $35
	Rogers	250MB: $15, 5GB: $35
	Telus	500MB: $20, 5GB: $35
U.K.	Orange	3GB: £15, 10GB: £25
	O2	1GB: £10, 2GB: £15
	Three	1GB: £10
	Vodafone	1GB: £10, 3GB: £15
France	Bouyguës	1GB: €30
	Orange	1GB: €27
	SFR	1GB: €35
Germany	Deutsche Telekom	3GB: €35
	O2	1GB: €15
	Vodafone	200MB: €15

Using Your iPad as a Hotspot

These days, many people carry multiple Internet-savvy devices: a smartphone, a laptop, and now an iPad. If you're using Wi-Fi, you can usually connect each device to the Internet individually, but doing so can mean paying for each device at a hotel, an airport lounge, or a café. And if you have no Wi-Fi available, then what?

The third-gen iPad might come to your rescue. (Sorry, not the earlier models.) It can act as a hotspot for other devices, meaning they can tap into your iPad's 3G or 4G connection to access the Internet. (This is also known as *tethering*.) After you connect the iPad to the Internet via 3G or 4G, you enable the Personal Hotspot feature in the Settings pane and then connect the other devices in any of three ways:

- Turn on the device's Wi-Fi and connect it to your iPad. (Your iPad's hotspot will appear in the other device's list of Wi-Fi access points.) On each device, you must enter the personal hotspot's password in the Settings app to ensure a stranger doesn't use your bandwidth unbeknownst to you.

- Turn on Bluetooth on both the iPad and the other devices and then pair them. (The process depends on each device's software.) Note that not all devices can be tethered via Bluetooth.

- Connect the iPad's 30-pin-to-USB cable between the iPad and a computer (sorry, not with other devices), and choose the iPad in the Mac's Network system preferences, in Windows 7's Network and Sharing Center control panel, or in Windows XP's Network Connections control panel.

Turn off the personal hotspot feature when it isn't in use so you don't accidentally eat through your data plan.

Not all carriers enable the iPad to work this way, but at press time, Verizon in the U.S. and Bell and Rogers in Canada were supporting the personal hotspot capability at no extra charge (though if you exceed your data cap, you'll need to buy another increment). The U.S.'s AT&T said it planned to support tethering but had not worked out the details. The U.K. carriers typically charge extra for tethering or require that you have a multiyear contract for surcharge-free tethering, but their plans were also in flux at press time.

TIP

Wi-Fi–only iPad owners who want to tap into 3G or 4G networks can try the Mi-Fi bridging devices sold by various carriers. The Mi-Fi taps into cellular networks and sends out a Wi-Fi signal for your iPad to use.

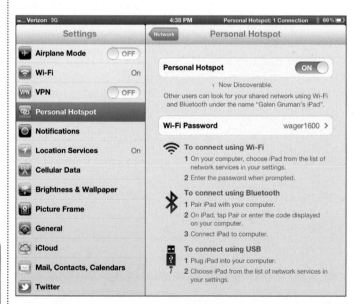

An iPad used as a personal hotspot. Note that the status bar turns blue and indicates the number of active connections.

DUMMIES

Syncing Files

- *Setting up iTunes*   ● *Syncing files to and from the iPad*

*i*Tunes is your master control station for backing up and syncing files — music, video, photos, books, apps, and even documents — between your computer and your iPad using either a Wi-Fi connection (in iOS 5) or the special USB cable-to-dock that comes with your iPad. To sync over Wi-Fi, choose the Sync with This iPad over Wi-Fi option in the Summary pane for your iPad in iTunes. You can also back up and sync data using Apple's iCloud service, as explained later in this section.

Some iPad applications can sync data between your computer and iPad — for example, PDF files in iBooks, text files in Quickoffice, and spreadsheets in iWork Numbers. To sync PDFs files with the iBooks app, for example, just drag the PDFs to the Books pane in iTunes on your computer. (Click Books in the Sidebar, below the Library label.) The PDFs will show up on your iPad the next time you sync it.

Telling iTunes What Files to Sync

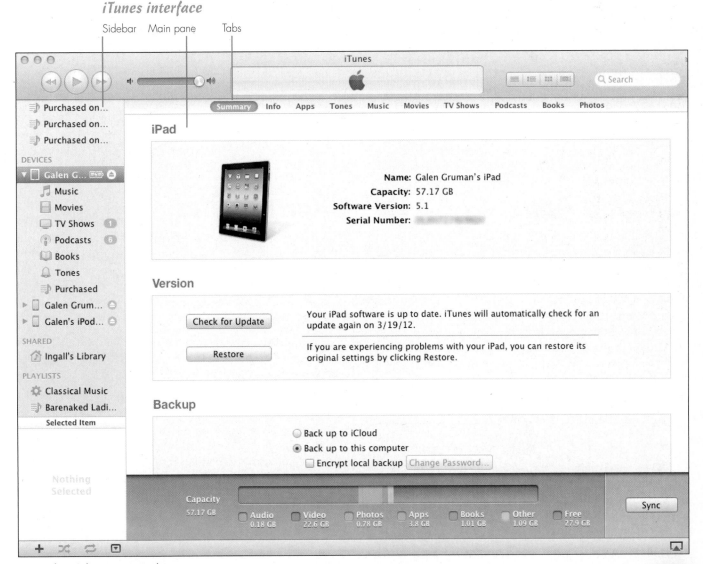

iTunes with an iPad's syncing options shown

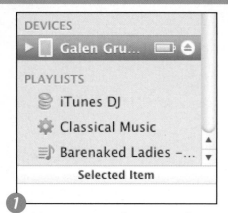

1 To customize what's synced in iTunes, click the iPad icon in the iTunes Sidebar's Devices list.

2 Click a tab at the top of the iTunes window and use the controls in the resulting pane to specify exactly what's synced to your iPad.

3 If you adjust the sync settings, click Apply in the lower-right corner of each pane to make the change, or click Revert to go back to the previous settings.

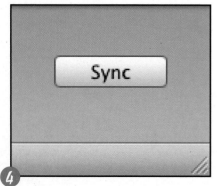

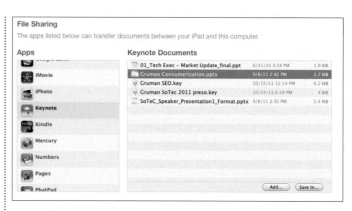

4 Click Sync each time you want to sync the computer and the iPad.

App-specific documents are visible in iTunes' Apps pane

Syncing Apps

When you're ready to transfer app data between your computer and your iPad apps, start in your computer's iTunes. In the Sidebar, look for your iPad's name and then select it. Go to the Apps pane and scroll to the bottom, where you see a list of applications. Click an app's name to see what documents it has on the iPad (as of the last time you synced). Drag documents from the pane to your desktop to copy them from the iPad, or drag them onto this pane from your computer to copy them to the iPad (and then sync the iPad to transfer them there).

REMEMBER

Unless you uncheck the Automatically Sync New Applications option at the bottom of the list, any apps you buy on your computer or on your iPad from the iTunes Store are automatically synced between the two devices.

Sharing Files

You have several ways to exchange data on your iPad with others. For example, you can e-mail photos from the iPad's Photos app and text from the Notes app by tapping their envelope-shaped icons. Many document-editing programs such as iWork, Quickoffice, and Documents to Go also let you e-mail documents to others.

You can also receive documents via e-mail. If a document type is supported, tap and hold its icon in the message. This opens the Open In menu, which lets you pick a compatible app to open it in.

Another option for syncing files is to use a cloud-based storage service such as iCloud, Google Drive (formerly called Google Docs), Dropbox, or Box. These services let you upload files from a computer to their Internet servers and then download them to the iPad, or vice versa.

For DUMMIES

Syncing with iCloud

Apple's iCloud service reduces your dependence on iTunes — and can even help eliminate it. iCloud includes a syncing service that keeps the music, books, apps, and TV shows and movies you buy via iTunes in sync across all your iOS 5 devices and computers tied to the same iTunes account. It also syncs images in your iPad Photos app's camera roll with iPhoto 9.2 and Aperture 3.2 or later on the Mac and the My Pictures folder in Windows, as well as with other iOS 5 devices' Photos app.

For all this to work, you need to enable iCloud on all the devices and computers you want to use it on. Here's how:

- In iOS, go to the Settings app, tap iCloud in the Sidebar, and tap Account to enter your Apple ID — the same one you use in the iTunes Store — and then tap Sign In. You see a list of services iCloud can sync. Use the switches to turn on the desired ones.

- In Mac OS X Lion (10.7.2 or later), be sure that iTunes has been updated to at least Version 10.5. Then go to the iCloud system preference, enter your Apple ID, tap Sign In, and then check the items you want to sync in the list that appears.

- In Windows Vista or 7, be sure to update iTunes to Version 10.5 or later. Then go to **www.apple.com/icloud**, download and install the iCloud control panel. (iCloud does not work in Windows XP.) In that control panel, sign in using your Apple ID and then check the items you want to sync in the list that appears. For bookmarks, click Options to choose whether to sync Internet Explorer or Safari bookmarks in Windows.

TIP

Mac OS X Lion 10.7.3 and iOS 5.1 have fixed a flaw in how mail, contacts, calendars, and notes are synced when you use a server-based e-mail system such as IMAP, Microsoft Exchange, or Google Apps/Gmail. Syncing such accounts via iCloud used to cause duplicate entries. Now it no longer does. But if you also sync these server-based services locally via the iTunes Info pane, you will get duplicates.

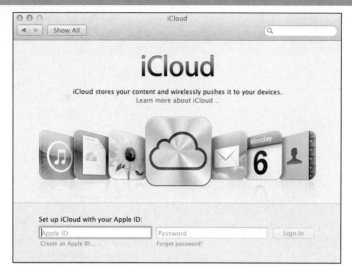

Backing up your iPad

Apple gives you two ways to back up your iPad: iTunes and iCloud. Both back up your iPad's settings, the Photos app's camera roll album, and documents to Apple's servers, so if you need to restore them, you don't need a computer. But only iTunes can back up movies and music, e-books, and other media you did not purchase through the iTunes Store. (iCloud will sync these items but not back them up for safekeeping.) The $24.99-per-year iTunes Match service will back up non-iTunes music to Apple's iCloud servers, as well as make them available to all your iOS devices.

You choose which backup method to use in iTunes' Summary pane for your iPad, or in the iCloud pane of the iPad's Settings app. Only one backup method can be enabled. And automatic backup occurs only if your iPad is plugged in to a power source, locked, and connected to the Internet via a Wi-Fi network.

If you use iCloud for backup, note that Apple provides 5GB of backup space at no charge. That space is used to store your settings, documents, and images in the Photos app's camera roll. Music and other media you buy through iTunes don't count against that storage — after all, Apple has to store them in its iTunes servers anyhow so customers can download them, so they are in essence already stored for you.

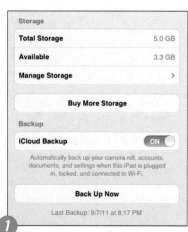

1 Manage your iCloud storage on the iPad by tapping Manage Storage in the Storage & Backup pane.

2 A list of devices being backed up displays, with the amount of data each is using.

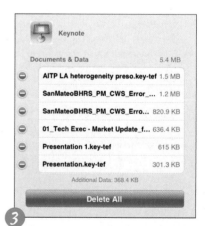

3 Tap any app to see a list of stored files, which you can then individually delete by tapping Edit and then the file's dash-in-a-red-circle icon.

Arranging the Display

In iTunes' Apps pane, you can rearrange app icons in iTunes by dragging them where you want them to appear on the iPad Home screens. (Be sure you've first selected your iPad from the Devices list in the Sidebar.) You can also select which apps are synced to your iPad by selecting or deselecting them from the iTunes list.

You can sort your apps by name, date, category, file size, or whether they are iPad-only apps by using the Sort By pop-up menu at the top of the list. Sorting your apps can make it easier to find the apps you want to sync or prevent from syncing.

App icon

(here, Archetype HD)

Drag icon

from Home Screen 7
to Home Screen 5

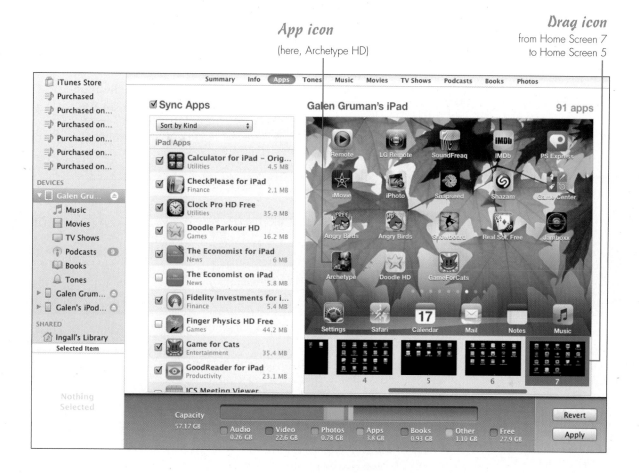

The wireless keyboard option

Apple and others sell Bluetooth-based wireless keyboards for the Mac that also work with the iPad. (One favorite is the Logitech Tablet Keyboard for iPad, shown here.) If you do extensive typing, they're faster than the onscreen keyboard, plus you can use shortcuts for copy and paste, but note that you'll often have to interrupt your typing to tap controls on the iPad's screen; you can't go all-keyboard. (You turn on Bluetooth in the Settings app's General pane.)

Searching Your iPad

A search feature in the iPad helps you find photos, music, e-mails, contacts, movies, and more — any data stored on your iPad, or accessible through your e-mail server. It's called universal search, and it's a great tool based on the Mac's Spotlight search capability.

REMEMBER

Despite the moniker *universal search*, Spotlight doesn't search everything: It won't search the web, your e-books, or the data stored in your apps (except for Contacts, Calendar, Mail, Notes, Reminders, Photos, Videos, and Music).

① To use Spotlight search, go to the Home screen by pressing the Home button.

② Swipe to the left until you see a mostly empty screen (the Spotlight screen) with a search box at the top labeled Search iPad.

③ Tap the Search iPad box, type in your search term, and tap Search on the onscreen keyboard or press Return if you're using a wireless physical keyboard.

④ Review the results. They show up below the Search iPad box and are organized by type (look for the icons at left), such as contacts, music (songs and albums), photos, videos, notes, e-mails, calendar appointments, and even application names.

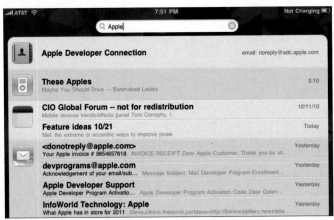

TIP

Instead of swiping to the left repeatedly, you can press the Home button (also repeatedly) until the Spotlight screen appears, ready to accept your search term. As you type your search term, the Spotlight screen may begin to show results based on what you type, even before you tap Search or press Return.

Running Apps

● *Running and switching among apps* ● *A tour of the 20 standard iPad apps* ● *Creating app groups*

The iPad's built-in apps

One of the iPad's most flexible capabilities is its support of applications, called *apps* by iPad users. The Home screen offers 20 built-in apps. To get to your Home screen, tap the Home button.

If your iPad is asleep when you tap, the unlock screen appears. After it's unlocked, you see whichever page of app icons was on the screen when your iPad went to sleep. If that was the Home screen, you're golden. If not, tap the Home button again to go to your iPad's main Home screen. (As you add apps, the iPad adds more Home screens — up to 11 — to hold them.)

To run an app, just tap it. To run a different app, press the Home button and then navigate to the new app and tap it.

To delete an app, tap and hold it until the app icons start to wiggle. Tap the icon of a white X in a black circle for the app you want to delete from your iPad. Tap the Home button to return to the normal iPad mode. That app is gone from your iPad but still available to re-download (for no cost) from the App Store if you ever want it back.

Rearranging Icons

1 Press and hold any icon until all the icons begin to wiggle.

2 Drag the icons around until you're happy with their positions. Don't tap the X-in-a-circle on an app icon, though — that deletes the app.

3 Press the Home button to save your arrangement and stop the wiggling.

Meet the Built-In Apps

If you haven't rearranged your icons, you see the following apps on the main Home screen:

✔ **Calendar:** If your computer's calendar program is Apple iCal, Google Calendar, Microsoft Entourage, or Microsoft Outlook, you can synchronize events and alerts with your iPad. It also syncs with Microsoft Exchange Apple iCloud, and Google Calendar servers.

✔ **Contacts:** This handy app contains information about the people you know. It syncs with Address Book, Entourage, or Outlook on your computer. It also syncs with Exchange and iCloud servers.

✔ **Notes:** This program enables you to type notes and send them by e-mail. You can set up your computer to sync notes automatically via Gmail or an IMAP or Microsoft Exchange e-mail server.

✔ **Maps:** View street maps or satellite imagery of locations around the globe, or ask for directions, traffic conditions, or even the location of a nearby pizza joint. If you have a Wi-Fi/cellular iPad, you can watch your location change as you move.

✔ **YouTube:** This app lets you watch videos from the popular YouTube website.

✔ **Videos:** This handy app is the repository for your movies, TV shows, and music videos.

✔ **iTunes:** Tap this app to purchase music, movies, TV shows, audiobooks, and more, and also download free podcasts and courses from iTunes U.

✔ **App Store:** Search the iTunes App Store for free and paid iPad apps to download. If any of your apps have updates, a red circle appears on the icon with a number of updates available.

✔ **Safari:** Safari is your browser, plain and simple.

✔ **Mail:** This application lets you send and receive e-mail with most POP3 and IMAP e-mail systems, as well as iCloud, Microsoft Hotmail, AOL, Yahoo!, Google's Gmail, and Microsoft Exchange.

✔ **Photos:** View pictures transferred from your camera or SD card reader (using the optional Camera Connection Kit) or from your computer. Zoom in or out, create slideshows, and e-mail photos.

✔ **Music:** Unleash all the power of an iPod on your iPad and listen to music or podcasts.

✔ **Game Center:** Access multiuser and other web-based games.

✔ **FaceTime** (except original iPad): Videoconference over Wi-Fi with iPad, iPhone, iPod touch, and Mac users.

✔ **Camera** (except original iPad): Take still photos and movies using the front or rear camera.

✔ **Messages:** Use this app to message with other iOS 5 users, (and, in summer 2012, Mac OS X Mountain Lion users) without paying SMS fees.

✔ **Newsstand:** A shortcut to magazine subscriptions purchased through the iTunes Store.

✔ **Photo Booth** (except original iPad): Apply often-silly special effects to your photos.

✔ **Reminders:** Track and manage tasks with this iOS 5 app.

✔ **Settings:** The central place for configuring your iPad, its services, and many of its apps.

From the top: Safari, Maps, Contacts, YouTube, and Photos

Switching among Apps

The iPad can run lots and lots of apps, and it lets you switch among them easily. Most people quickly learn that pressing the Home button when they're in an app returns them to the Home screen, from which they can tap another app to open it. But there are easier ways to switch among running apps than going through the Home screen.

One option is to double-press the Home button to open the multitasking bar: This action causes a scrollable row of icons to appear at the bottom of the screen. Scroll to the left to get the controls over audio and video playback and set the rotation lock or mute the iPad. (If the side switch is set to rotation lock, the mute control appears here; if the side switch is set to mute, the rotation control appears here.) Scroll to the right to see all running apps, and tap the one you want to switch to. They're listed in order of most recent use.

You can also use gestures if the Multitasking Gestures switch is set to On in the Settings app's General pane. Scroll up with four fingers to open the multitasking bar, and scroll down with four fingers to close it. Or scroll to the right or left with four fingers to move among the running apps.

Switch among apps using the four-finger horizontal scroll gesture

Creating Groups

Your 11 Home screens can fill up fast if you're not careful, so you might want to group your apps to keep them together and minimize the number of Home screens to scroll through.

To do that, tap and hold any app icon to cause the apps to wiggle. Drag an app onto another app you want in the same group. iOS creates a group containing the two apps. Drag additional apps into the group. The group's name is based on the type of app you started with, but simply tap its name at the top of the group window to edit it. When you tap a group icon, the group window opens, and you tap any of its apps to open that app. Tap outside the group to close the window if you decide not to launch one of its apps. (If you do run one of its apps, the group window closes automatically.)

The multitasking bar (at bottom) lets you switch among running apps.

An app group

Common Capabilities

● *Setting notification* ● *Printing* ● *Taking dictation*

The built-in Spotlight search capability explained earlier isn't the only system service the iPad's iOS offers. Other common capabilities include the ability for apps to notify you of alerts and new information, to print to compatible printers, and, on the third-generation iPad, even to take dictation.

It's these kinds of built-in capabilities that let iOS apps do so much more, because their developers can just use what Apple has built and focus their efforts on their apps' specialty capabilities.

Getting Notified As You Like

Introduced in iOS 5, the Notification Center lets you know when you get new messages, tweets, or any alerts for the software you allow to notify you. You specify in the Settings app which apps' notifications are brought to your attention, as well as how they are made visible. The options are

Specifying how a notification displays for an app

✔ **Badge:** The number in a red circle that appears on an app icon on the Home screen indicating the number of alerts for that app.

✔ **Banner:** A brief alert that appears at the top of the screen for a few seconds. Tap it while it's visible to open the app and its message.

✔ **Alert:** A panel that appears in the center of the screen containing the alert message. It interrupts what you're doing, so you should use it only for apps with urgent alerts. You get the option to close the alert or go to the app.

For each app, you can also set whether you get a preview of the message itself (such as the first few words of a tweet or e-mail), how many alerts from that app are displayed, whether and how often its alerts repeat, and whether its alerts are visible on the lock screen.

You can see notifications at any time by swiping down from the status bar to pull down the Notification Center's tray.

The Notification Center's pull-down tray (top) and the notification panel on the lock screen (bottom)

Dictation on the Third-Gen iPad

Even with its full-size onscreen keyboard and the option to use a Bluetooth physical keyboard with an iPad, some people dream of a more *Star Trek*–like relationship where they can simply talk to the iPad, much like is possible with the iPhone 4S's Siri service. Sadly, there's as yet no Siri for iPad, but the third-gen iPad brings the next best thing: dictation. (Sorry, owners of previous iPads!)

To enable dictation for use in any app that allows text entry, you need to do two things:

- Turn on the Dictation switch in the Keyboard pane of the Settings app's General pane.

- Have a live connection to the Internet (either Wi-Fi or cellular). Without such a connection, dictation is unavailable because the iPad sends a recording of your speech to Apple's servers, which do the heavy lifting of speech-to-text translation and then send the results back to the iPad.

Enable Dictation in the Keyboard pane of the Settings app's General pane.

From iPad to Paper

In this electronic age, the need to print keeps decreasing — you can even board an airplane using your smartphone, after all, rather than have a printed boarding pass. But there are times when having a paper copy comes in very handy. iOS lets you print from your iPad, if you have a compatible AirPrint printer connected to your home or business network.

With such a printer available, many apps provide the Print menu option from their Share menu. Tap it and then specify the printer and numbers of copies desired. Some applications, such as Apple's Pages, Numbers, and Keynote, provide the Print option from other menus (in these apps' case, from the Tools menu).

The Print option in Mail

1 When dictation is enabled, you'll see a new key on the onscreen keyboard: the Dictate key. (It looks like an old-fashioned microphone.)

2 Tap the Dictate key and begin speaking. It changes color and throbs as it hears you. (If you're silent too long, dictation turns itself off.)

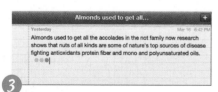

3 Tap the Dictate key when you're done. Wait a few seconds (three large dots appear where your text will be inserted), and then you'll see the results.

You can now dictate text into any field or app that you can type in; you don't have to dictate into a specific app and then copy and paste the results where you want to use them. Be sure to speak clearly and in a level voice to minimize the misinterpretations inevitable with speech-to-text translation. As your fourth-grade teacher no doubt commanded, "Enunciate!"

TIP

If you don't have an AirPrint-compatible printer, consider buying the $149 xPrintServer made by Lantronix. Plug it into your network and voilà!; most of your printers connected to the network become AirPrint-compatible. Although pricey for a home, it's a great option for an office or school, and for a larger business that has a network administrator, EFI's PrintMe Mobile software for Windows Server also makes most network printers AirPrint-compatible (and compatible with Google Android mobile devices as well).

Multi-Touch Basics

● *Learning the iPad's touch gestures* ● *Copying text and graphics*

The iPad uses a touchscreen technology — on a Multi-Touch display — which means that when you swipe your finger across the screen or tap an icon, you're providing input (called a gesture) to the device. Use the pads of your fingertips (not fingernails) to make the gestures.

Tap and hold to insert the text cursor in a specific location in text. When you do so, a magnifying orb appears over the selected text, so you can more easily see the cursor location. With your finger still held down, move your finger within the text to the desired location. Release your finger when the text cursor is where you want it to be. This technique works not only when working with text in e-mails and notes but also in search boxes, URL fields, and any element in which you can type text.

Gesture	What You Can Do with It
Double-tap	Enlarge or reduce the display of a web page or zoom in or out in the Maps app. Other apps may also zoom when you double-tap within them. Select text or graphics for cutting, copying, or pasting.
Drag	Scroll through a screen or page as you drag a finger.
Flick (quickly swipe)	Scroll through web pages, app screens, and the like when you flick a finger onscreen in the direction you want to move. Get a Delete button on an e-mail message by flicking to the left or right.
Pinch	Zoom in on the screen by pinching two fingers together while looking at photos, maps, web pages, or e-mail messages.
Scroll	Drag a finger in the direction you want to scroll the screen of an app or a web page. Note that you may need to drag two fingers to scroll within the screen, such as for a list or pane.
Expand	Zoom out by spreading two fingers onscreen.
Swipe	Move to the next Home screen by swiping a finger or two from right to left on the screen. Swipe from left to right to move the other way.
Tap	Open an app from the Home screen by tapping its icon. Move quickly to the top of a list, a web page, or an e-mail message by tapping the status bar. Move the cursor to a location in text (such as in an e-mail or a search box) by tapping the location. Activate an object (such as a hyperlink, list item, or button) by tapping it.
Tap and hold	Get the Open In menu to open a file attachment (tap and hold it) in another app. Get the option to open a link in a new window when you tap and hold it.
Twist	Rotate an object by twisting two fingers in apps that support such rotation.

Pinch and expand gestures zoom in and out.

iOS 5 adds new navigation gestures (be sure Multitasking Gestures is on in the Settings app's General pane):

• Swipe up with four fingers to open the multitasking bar.

• Swipe left or right with four fingers to navigate among running apps.

• Pinch with three fingers and your thumb to open the Home screen when in an app.

Select, Cut, Copy, and Paste

Being able to select and then copy and paste text or images from one place on a computer to another has seemingly been a divine right, and that's the case on the iPad as well. You might copy text or images from the web and paste them into an e-mail or a note. Or, you might copy a bunch of pictures or video into an e-mail. On the iPad, you can copy and paste (and cut) with pizzazz.

Double-tap a word or graphic to select it. A menu appears above the selection, and when you select a word, you have choices:

✔ Tap Select to select the adjacent word.

✔ Tap Select All to grab everything.

✔ Tap and hold to get the selection handles, which you then drag to select the text.

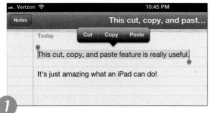

1 After you've selected the text, tap Copy or Cut in the new menu that appears. In some cases, you can also tap Replace to substitute previously copied text for the words you've selected. If a possibly misspelled word is selected, the Suggest option may appear. And in some apps, the Define option may appear when you select individual words.

2 When you decide where to insert the text or graphic you just cut or copied — in the current app or in another one — tap and hold at the desired insertion point.

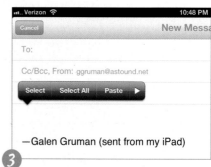

3 Up pops a menu with commands that may include Select, Select All, Replace, and Paste. Tap Paste to paste the selection.

Copy items other than text

When selecting graphics to copy, double-tap, or in some apps tap and hold, to get the menu. You can also press and hold the Phone or Address fields in the iPad Contacts app, or a link in Safari, and use the Copy button to copy the selection.

What's New in the Third-Gen iPad

Apple continues to push the technology envelope in the iPad. The latest version, the third-generation iPad (also called the iPad 3 and the iPad HD), takes several innovations from the iPhone 4 and iPhone 4S — the high-resolution Retina display and the dictation portion of the Siri voice-recognition system, respectively — and adds its own new capability: support for 4G LTE networks, which run about two to four times as fast as the 3G networks of the previous iPads and current iPhones. You get more image and text clarity and more Internet speed as a result.

Amazingly, the iPad's battery life remains in its predecessors' 9- to 11-hour range, the weight is just 0.1 pounds more (1.5 pounds), and the dimensions are just a hair thicker (so, if you're an upgrader, your iPad 2's Smart Cover and protective skins still fit). Apple has also juiced up the graphics-processing power in the third-gen iPad's new A5X processor, which means games, photo editors, and more can zip along with the larger, higher-resolution images on the new iPad.

- **Retina display:** The most visible improvement to the third-gen iPad is the high-resolution display, which doubles the number of pixels from 1,024 x 768 to 2,048 x 1,536. That means much clearer text, more natural color balance, and fewer artifacts when watching HD videos (think of it as the iPad's version of Blu-ray), greater detail control in photo editors, and hyper-realistic animations in games.

- **HD camera:** The new iPad's rear camera got a big boost in resolution as well, now capturing 5 megapixels (up from just 0.7 megapixels for photos in the iPad 2) and able to shoot 1080p HD video (up from 720p in the iPad 2). Better image sensors and the larger (f/2.4) aperture also allow for low-light-level photography. (The front camera is unchanged from the iPad 2 design.)

An HD video on the third-gen iPad's Retina display (top), compared to a previous iPad (bottom). Note the finer detail and more natural-looking colors on the Retina display.

A close-up of a card game optimized for the Retina display (left) shows greater detail for the peacock and smoother rendering of the cards compared to the same game in a previous iPad (right).

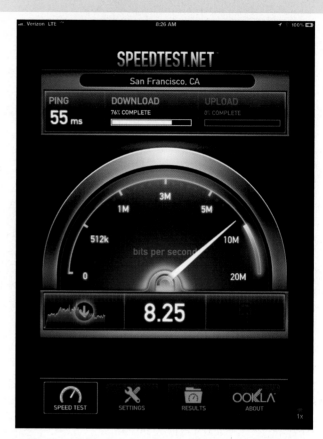

On the 4G model of the third-gen iPad, you can get blazing Internet speeds where available — comparable to your home's broadband speeds.

✔ **4G LTE:** Available as an option at the time of purchase, the LTE radio gives you fast Internet connectivity wherever your carrier provides 4G service. When 4G is unavailable, you get the fast-enough 3G speed that all cellular tablets and smartphones rely on.

✔ **Personal hotspot:** For carriers that allow it, the 4G iPad models let you share your cellular Internet connection with computers and other devices. You go online on the cellular service and then have the other devices connect to your iPad via Wi-Fi, Bluetooth, or (for computers only) a cable.

✔ **Global roaming:** All new 4G iPad models, not just those based on the GSM cellular technology, now let you pop in a MicroSIM from a local carrier when you're in a foreign country, so you get local access at lower prices. Bye-bye, high data-roaming charges!

✔ **Bluetooth 4.0:** The short-range Bluetooth wireless technology often used for wireless headsets and streaming audio to a car stereo has earned a rep for being slow and power-hungry. The new iPad uses the new Bluetooth 4.0 standard that ups the speed and reduces the battery usage, allowing more reliable and longer sessions with other Bluetooth 4-compatible devices.

✔ **Dictation:** When you have an Internet connection, the iPad can take dictation, entering what you say into any application or field that allows text input. Tap the Dictate key (the microphone icon), say your piece, tap the key again, and

the iPad sends off your recording to Apple's servers for speech-to-text translation and then enters the results for you. (Enable dictation in the Keyboard pane of the Settings app's General pane.)

What's New in iOS 5.1

The third-gen iPad's debut also marked the debut of the iOS 5.1 update, which is also available for earlier iPad models. In addition to enabling dictation and the personal hotspot capabilities in the third-gen iPad, it brings a few minor improvements to iPads and iPhones.

The Photos app now lets you delete images in iCloud's Photo Stream syncing service, so you can delete them from the iPad and have them deleted on all devices connected to the same iCloud account and that have Photo Stream enabled.

The Camera app has a new arrangement of its onscreen buttons but no new capabilities.

iOS 5.1 also lets iCloud sync iTunes-purchased movies to the iPad and other devices, just as iOS 5.0 enabled syncing of music, e-books, and apps. You'll need a Wi-Fi connection, however, because the files are too large to transmit over 3G or 4G networks.

Taking a Web Safari

A version of the Apple Safari web browser is a major reason that the web on the iPad is very much like the web you've come to expect on a more traditional computer. Come to think of it, the web often looks a lot better on the iPad thanks to its beautiful screen. The iPad's glorious display, in combination with the snappy Apple-designed A4 chip inside the original iPad, and even faster A5 in the iPad 2 and third-gen iPad, makes browsing on Apple's tablet an absolute delight.

Safari for the Mac (and for Windows) is one of the best web browsers in the business. Likewise, Safari on the iPhone has no rival as a smartphone browser. And as you might imagine, Safari on the iPad is equally appealing.

Getting on the Internet with your iPad is easy using its Wi-Fi or optional cellular capabilities. When you're online, Safari is your ticket to a wide world of information, entertainment, education, and more. Safari will be familiar to you if you've used it on a Mac or PC, though the way you move around will be new to you due to the iPad's gesture-based touchscreen interface.

Using the Onscreen Keyboard

Surfing the web begins with a web address, or URL, of course. When you start by tapping the address field in the iPad's Safari app, the onscreen keyboard appears. Because so many web addresses end with the suffix *.com,* the onscreen keyboard has a dedicated .com key. For other common web suffixes, tap and hold the .com key and choose the relevant domain type (.edu, .net, or .org, plus country-specific domains, such as .us and .fr, based on the iPad's language settings). Both the period (.) and the slash (/) appear on the onscreen keyboard in Safari because you frequently use them to enter web addresses.

TIP

The moment you tap a single letter in Safari's address field, you see a list of web addresses that match the letter based on your prior entries (history) and bookmarks. For example, if you tap the letter *E,* you see web listings for *EarthLink, eBay,* and others. Tapping *U* or *H* instead may display listings for *USA Today* or the *Houston Chronicle,* respectively. As you type more letters, the suggestions narrow to those with that text. To go to any of the suggestions, just tap it.

How Mobile Safari Differs

Using Safari on an iPad is very much like using it on a computer: You enter the web addresses you want to visit or go to the bookmarks to quickly visit favorite sites. You can search the web using your choice of Google, Yahoo!, and Bing. And you have the Back, Forward, and Reload buttons of any browser.

But Safari for the iPad has some key differences with a desktop browser that you should know up front:

- There is no Home button on the browser, so you can't set a default web page.

- You navigate and zoom pages using gestures, not via a keyboard, a mouse, or scroll bars.

- You're limited to nine browser tabs for containing open web pages, and you can't open new browser windows as on the desktop.

 You can easily e-mail the current page's web address to anyone by tapping the Share button and then choosing Mail Link to This Page. Likewise, if you've specified your Twitter account in the Settings app, you can choose Tweet to send the URL and a brief message to your Twitter followers.

- You can save websites as icons on your Home screen — not just bookmark them — by choosing Add to Home Screen from the Share menu.

Because the iPad runs iOS, the same operating system used for the smaller-screen iPhone, every so often you may run into a site that serves up the light, or mobile, version of a website, sometimes known as a WAP site. Graphics may be stripped down on these sites. Alas, the site producers may be unwittingly discriminating against you for dropping in on them by using an iPad. (Some give you a choice by providing a link to the full, or desktop, version of the site; if so, use it!)

Smart Safety Settings

Along with the riches found on the web are places where you're hassled and you might want to protect your privacy and maintain your security. To get started, tap the Settings app's icon on the Home screen. Now tap Safari. You have these options:

✔ **AutoFill:** When AutoFill is turned on, Safari can automatically fill out web forms by using your personal contact information, usernames and passwords, or information from other contacts in your address book.

✔ **Private Browsing:** Turn this option on so your browsing history and search history are not saved, so other users can't see what you've been doing in Safari. (Note that the toolbars switch from light gray to dark gray when private browsing is on.)

✔ **Accept Cookies:** *Cookies* are tiny bits of information that a website places in a browser when you visit so that the site recognizes you when you return. Most cookies are benign, and you have control: Tap Accept Cookies and then tap Never, From Visited (a reasonable setting), or Always. ***Note:*** If you don't let the iPad accept cookies, some web pages won't load properly.

✔ **Clear History** and **Clear Cookies and Data:** The history stores the website addresses you've visited recently. Cookies store information that helps the site remember you, and the cache stores content from some web pages so that they load faster the next time you stop by. Delete any of this stored information by tapping its button and then tapping Clear.

✔ **Fraud Warning:** Safari can warn you when you land on a site whose producers have sinister intentions. The protection is better than nothing, but don't give up your guard: Fraud Warning isn't foolproof.

✔ **JavaScript:** Programmers use JavaScript to add various kinds of functionality to web pages, from displaying the date and time to changing images when you mouse over them.

✔ **Block Pop-Ups:** Pop-ups are those web pages that show up whether or not you want them to. Often, they're annoying advertisements. But at some sites, you may welcome the appearance of pop-ups, so remember to turn off blocking when at those sites.

✔ **Website Data:** These supersize cookies store information on your iPad so a website doesn't have to keep loading when you visit. Tap Advanced and then Website Data to see the databases on your iPad; tap any database to see how much data it's storing. To delete a website's data, tap the Edit button in the upper-right corner, tap the white – (minus) icon (it's in a red circle), and then tap the Delete button that appears.

Searching the Web

Most people spend a lot of time using search engines on the web. If you don't know the address of the site you want to visit (or you want to research a topic or find something you need online), you'll find it quickly with Safari's search feature. By default, Safari uses the Google search engine, with Yahoo! and Microsoft Bing as options.

You can certainly use the onscreen keyboard to type **google.com, yahoo.com,** or **bing.com** in the Safari address field, but Apple doesn't require that tedious effort. Instead, just tap into Google, Yahoo!, or Bing by using the Safari search box.

Just tap the search box, type in your search terms, and tap the keyboard's Search button. You'll get a results page — just like you do on your computer's browser. Tap any result that looks interesting (be sure to scroll down to see all the results), and if you don't find useful results, go to the next page of the search results or try a different search term.

To switch the search box to Yahoo! or Bing (or back to Google), tap Settings on the Home screen, scroll down, tap Safari, tap Search Engine, and then tap to choose one search behemoth over the other.

If you use Google for search, you can browse for specific items such as images, videos, and maps by tapping any of the links at the top of the Google results window. Also, tap the Advanced Search link to the right of the Google results page's Search button to specify more search details and narrow your search. Yahoo! and Bing have similar options on their results pages.

*Just **tap into Google**, Yahoo!, or Bing by using the Safari **search box***

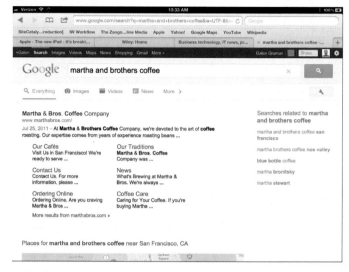

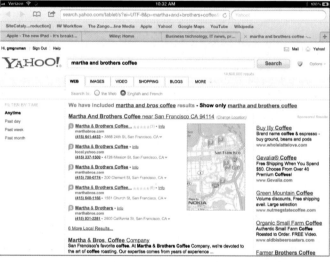

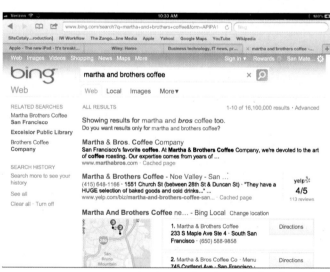

Search engines from the top: Google, Yahoo!, and Bing

Keep Your Browsing Private

A fact of life on the web is that most activity is monitored and tracked so providers can better understand users' preferences and, of course, make suggestions on what they might want to buy. Even though that tracking is often anonymous, the potential exists for your activities to be discovered.

And it's not usually websites that cause tracking concerns. That Safari history feature in its Bookmarks menu that I explain in the next article? Anyone with access to your iPad can see that history and see where you've been. That could be embarrassing if your iPad is shared with others.

One way to reduce that tracking is to disable cookies, as explained earlier in this section. But many websites won't work when cookies are disabled. And disabled cookies don't turn off the history feature of bookmarks. So a better option to safeguard your browser privacy is to enable Safari's Private Browsing feature, which you do in the Safari pane of the Settings app.

When the Private Browsing switch is set to On, your web history is no longer recorded by Safari — you can look at the history list and see that nothing is added when you're in this mode. You can tell you've enabled private browsing because the Safari toolbar turns dark gray.

Safari's toolbar goes dark gray when private browsing is enabled.

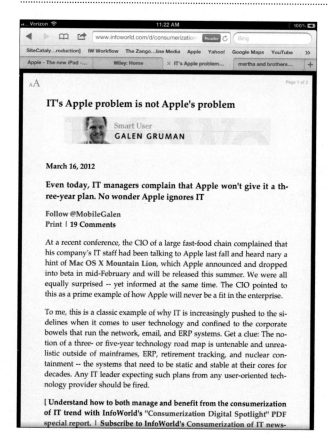

Safari's Reader mode

Simplify Your Reading

You may notice the gray Reader icon that appears to the right of the URL in Safari when you visit some pages. That's an indication the website supports Safari's Reader view, which strips out everything but the main text. You can even change the text size by tapping the AA button at the upper left of the Reader window that appears when you tap the Reader icon. (Safari for Mac OS X and Windows has the same feature, but not Safari for the iPhone.)

While you're in Reader mode, the Reader button turns purple, but I suspect you'll know even without that visual clue because of how dramatically different the web page looks. ***Note:*** Turning on Reader mode doesn't affect any other web pages you have open in other tabs, and if you open a different web page in a tab where Reader is active, that new page doesn't have reader turned on for it automatically.

TIP

If you print when in Reader mode, the web page's contents are formatted like a printed page, complete with page numbers and the typical portrait orientation of paper pages (even if you're holding the iPad horizontally).

Bookmarking Pages

● *Adding, editing, and accessing bookmarks* ● *Tracing your browser history* ● *Creating web clips*

1 f you use a computer, you already know how useful bookmarks are to access favorite web pages in your browser. And you may also use the browser's history feature to find pages you visited but didn't bookmark. Safari on the iPad offers the same capabilities.

You can transfer your computer's bookmarks (if you use Safari or Internet Explorer) to your iPad, so you don't have to re-enter them all. When you sync your iPad in iTunes on the Mac, be sure that Sync Safari Bookmarks is selected

*You can **transfer** … bookmarks … when you **sync in iTunes***

in the Other section inside the Info pane for your iPad. In Windows, select Sync Bookmarks From and then choose Safari or Internet Explorer, as appropriate. Alternatively, you can use iCloud to sync bookmarks instead.

Even better, the next time you sync, any bookmarks added on your iPad are transferred to your computer, just as any bookmarks added on your computer are transferred to your iPad. The process for working with bookmarks on the iPad's Safari app is very similar to what you would do on a computer's browser.

To add bookmarks in Safari, follow these steps:

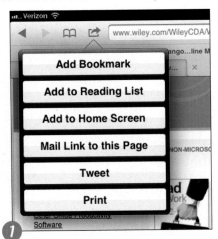

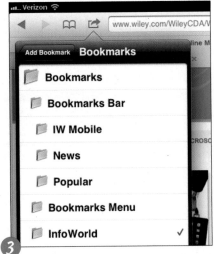

1 Make sure that the page you want to bookmark is open and tap the Share button at the top of the browser. A menu appears with several options; tap Add Bookmark.

2 The Add Bookmark menu opens with a default name for the bookmark, its web address, and its folder location. To accept the defaults, tap Save.

To change the default bookmark name, tap the X icon, enter the new title (using the onscreen keyboard), and then tap Save.

3 If you want to specify a different folder for the bookmark you're adding, tap the folder name displayed at the bottom of the Add Bookmark menu to get a list of all folders and then tap the desired one. Or, if you don't want to change the folder after all, tap the Add Bookmark button at the top left of the menu.

The Add Bookmark menu reverts to the form shown in Step 2. Tap Save to save the bookmark in the specified folder.

You can constantly display a bookmarks bar in Safari by turning on the Always Show Bookmarks Bar setting in the Settings app's Safari pane.

Choose Add to Reading List to save an article you want to read later. Safari removes it from the list once you've read it.

Managing Bookmarks

To open a bookmarked page after you set it up, tap the Bookmarks button in the upper-left portion of the Safari window and then tap the appropriate bookmark. If the bookmark you have in mind is buried inside a folder, tap the folder name first and then tap the bookmark you want.

The bookmarks list of folders and pages before (left) and after (right) tapping Edit

If a bookmarked site is no longer meaningful, you can change it or get rid of it:

- **To remove a bookmark (or folder),** tap the Bookmarks icon and then tap Edit. Tap the icon of a – (minus) in a red circle next to the bookmark you want to delete, and then tap Delete.

- **To change a bookmark name or location,** tap Edit and then tap the bookmark. The Edit Bookmark screen appears, showing the name, web address, and location of the bookmark already filled in. Tap the fields you want to change.

- **To create a new folder for your bookmarks,** tap Edit and then tap the New Folder button. Enter the name of the new folder and choose where to put it.

- **To move a bookmark up or down in a list,** tap Edit and then drag the three bars to the right of the bookmark's name to its new resting place.

Saving Web Clips

You frequent lots of websites; you're constantly going online to consult your daily train schedule, for example. The folks at Apple let you bestow special privileges on frequently visited sites, not just by bookmarking pages but by affording them their unique home screen icons. Apple calls these *web clips*.

Creating a web clip is easy: Tap the Action button (curved-arrow icon) in Safari and choose Add to Home Screen. A dialog box appears in which you can edit the name for the icon that will be placed on the Home screen. The icon is then added to your Home screen, where you can manage it like any app icon.

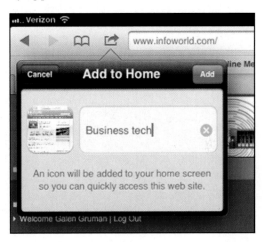

Revisiting History

Sometimes, you want to revisit a site that you failed to bookmark, but you can't remember the darn destination or what led you there in the first place. Fortunately, as you move around the web, Safari keeps a record of your browsing history, saving several days' worth of visits.

History within the Bookmarks menu

Here's how to access your history:

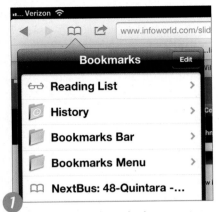

① Tap the Bookmarks button. A menu appears.

② At the top of the menu, tap History. You then get a list of the most recent visits at top and then several folders containing previous days' visits.

③ If you see the site you want, tap it. Otherwise, tap the folder for the day you think you last visited the site you want. When you find the site, tap it to open the page.

Sharing Web Goodies

While you're surfing the web on your iPad, you may run across a great site or graphic that you want to share. You can do so easily by sending the graphic or a link to the site in an e-mail or tweet.

You can easily copy a graphic in a web page. Just tap and hold on the graphic for a menu to appear. Tap Save Image to save the graphic to the Photos app. If you tap Copy instead, you can paste the image into an e-mail or other image-capable app — but note that if the graphic is set up as a link on the web page, tapping Copy copies its link, not the graphic itself.

TIP

If you have more than one e-mail or Twitter account set up on the iPad, you can choose which account to send the message from by tapping the From field and choosing one of your accounts.

① Tap the Share button; then choose Mail Link to This Page or Tweet, depending on how you want to share the URL.

② In the Mail app, a message window opens that has the web address included in the message text. Address the e-mail to your desired recipients, add a subject, and enter any additional text in the message body. In Twitter, add any tweet text as well.

③ Tap Send to deliver the message.

Setting Up E-Mail

IN THIS ARTICLE

- *Configuring various accounts*
  - *Changing your mail settings*

1 t's an activity that most people do every day on their computers and smartphones — and one you can do on your iPad. That activity is reading and sending e-mail. The iPad's built-in Mail app lets you do e-mail from all the accounts you have. The Mail app can handle not just text e-mails but rich HTML e-mail messages — those formatted with font and type styles and embedded graphics. If someone sends you e-mail with a picture, it's visible right in the body of the message.

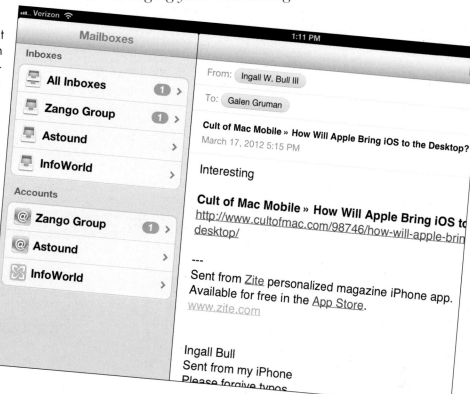

Furthermore, Mail can display several types of file attachments, including (but not limited to) PDFs, JPEG images, Microsoft Word documents, PowerPoint slides, and Excel spreadsheets, as well as stuff produced through Apple's own iWork software. Better still, all this sending and receiving of text, graphics, and documents can happen in the background so that you can surf the web or play a game while your iPad quietly and efficiently handles your e-mail behind the scenes.

...e-mail from all the accounts you have

First things first: To use Mail, you need an e-mail account. Maybe you have one at work that you want to access via your iPad. You probably have one or more personal e-mail accounts, such as those that are usually issued with broadband Internet access (that is, a cable modem, fiber-optic, or DSL) or ones you may have set up for free from Yahoo!, Google, MSN, or numerous other service providers.

TIP

Some outgoing mail servers don't need your username and password. That's why the fields for these items on your iPad note that they're optional. If you fill in your username and password and find that the server is unable to send your e-mail, try removing them from these fields.

Setting Up Accounts

The first time you launch Mail, you see the Welcome to Mail screen. If you've previously set up an e-mail account and want to add a new one, do so by going to the Settings app; tapping the Mail, Contacts, Calendars option; and tapping Add Account. Then tap the account type you want to add to the iPad; your choices are iCloud, Microsoft Exchange, Gmail, Yahoo!, AOL, Hotmail, MobileMe, and Other.

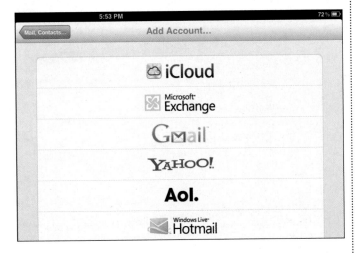

Popular e-mail accounts

If you're setting up an iCloud, MobileMe, Gmail, Yahoo!, Hotmail, Mail, or AOL account, you get a dialog box in which you enter a descriptive name for the account (such as **Bob's Gmail**), your name, your e-mail address, and the e-mail account's password. Tap Save, and you're done.

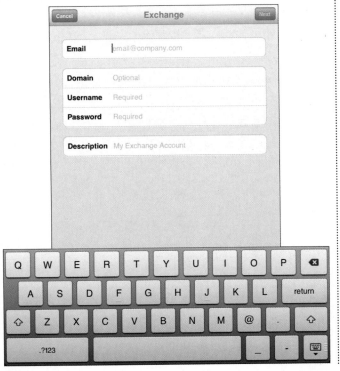

The iPad lets you access e-mail from pretty much any e-mail account — and you can set up more than one account on your iPad.

IMAP and POP accounts

You may get your e-mail through some other provider — an IT department, your Internet service provider, or someone else — that uses one of the two e-mail server technologies (called *protocols*): IMAP and POP. To set up such accounts, start by tapping the Other button in the Add Account screen. Under Mail, tap Add Mail Account.

Fill in the name, address, password, and description in the appropriate fields. Tap Save. With any luck, that's all you have to do. The iPad tries to retrieve your account credentials. If it finds them, you're done. Otherwise, you need some additional information that your e-mail service provider can help you with.

Adding the provider's e-mail details

If your iPad can't figure out the connection, check your e-mail service documentation or ask your e-mail provider for the following information:

- The type of e-mail server this account uses: IMAP or POP.

- The Internet host name for your incoming mail server, usually *mail.providername.com,* and the associated username and password. (Replace *providername* with the actual domain for your provider.)

- The Internet host name for your outgoing mail server, which is often *smtp.providername.com,* and the associated username and password.

Enter all these details and then tap the Save button in the upper-right corner to create the account.

Corporate e-mail

The iPad easily works with the Microsoft Exchange e-mail servers that are a staple in large enterprises, as well as many smaller businesses. Setting up Exchange e-mail isn't particularly taxing, and the iPad connects to Exchange right out of the box. But you still might have to consult your employer's techie types for certain settings.

If your company uses Lotus Notes, use IBM's Lotus Notes Traveler app to get e-mail, calendars, and contacts on your iPad. Novell GroupWise users will need the Novell Data Synchronizer Mobility Pack installed on their server.

Start setting up your Exchange e-mail with these steps:

Select Exchange services to enable.

1 In the Settings app, tap Mail, Contacts, Calendars and then tap Add Account.

2 Tap the Microsoft Exchange icon on the Add Account screen.

3 Fill in what you can: your e-mail address, domain (if used), username (sometimes entered as **domain\user**), and password. Or, call on your IT staff for assistance. Tap Next.

4 Choose which information you want to synchronize through Exchange by sliding the Mail, Contacts, Calendars, or Reminders switches to On. Tap Save.

REMEMBER

If the Microsoft autodiscovery service can't complete your setup for you (after Step 3), a screen appears asking for additional information, such as the server address. That server address may begin with *exchange.company.com* or *webmail.company.com*. Ask your IT staff for help if needed. Tap Next when you're done.

Setting Mail Options

You can customize how the iPad behaves when receiving, displaying, and sending e-mail, all from the Settings app. Go to the Mail, Contacts, Calendars pane's Mail section to set the options you see in the table.

Option	What You Do	Selections
How many messages show for each account	Tap Show	25, 50, 75, 100, or 200
How many message lines display in the list	Tap Preview	None, 1, 2, 3, 4, or 5
Text size for messages	Tap Minimum Font Size	Small, Medium, Large, Extra Large, or Giant
To or Cc recipient indicator	Slide Show To/Cc Label	On or Off
Confirmation dialog box (when you delete messages)	Slide Ask Before Deleting	On or Off
Load images embedded from a website	Slide Load Remote Images	On or Off
Display messages by thread (not by date)	Slide Organize by Thread	On or Off
Hear a message-sent alert	Tap Sounds (in the General pane) and slide Sent Mail	On or Off
Addition of a signature line, phrase, or block of text to sent messages	Tap Signature	The default signature ("Sent from my iPad"), edited as desired
Receipt of a copy of every sent message	Slide Always Bcc Myself	On or Off
Default account for sending e-mail	Tap Default Account	The list of e-mail accounts you set up
Indent previous message's text in a message reply	Tap Increase Quote Level	On or Off

WARNING!

On PCs, especially Windows ones, remote images can be used to infect the PCs with viruses. It's possible on an iPad as well, although so far hackers have stayed focused on Windows.

TIP

You can tell the iPad to get more messages than the maximum you set here. Just scroll to the bottom of your message list and tap Load More Messages — just like on the iPhone. (For an Exchange account, go to the account in the Settings app and then tap Mail Days to Sync to select how far back to keep messages on your iPad.)

What's up with Exchange ActiveSync?

If your company supports something known as Microsoft Exchange ActiveSync, you can exploit *push e-mail* so that messages arrive pronto on the iPad, just as they do on your other computers. (To keep everything up to date, the iPad also supports push calendars and push contacts.) For push to work, your company must be running Microsoft Exchange 2003 (Service Pack 2), 2007 (Service Pack 1), or 2010. Ask your company's IT or tech department if you run into an issue.

ActiveSync also lets your company enforce its security requirements on your iPad for Exchange, corporate Gmail, and other e-mail systems. That helps businesses allow iPads to access their networks.

FOR DUMMIES

Working with E-Mails

IN THIS ARTICLE

- *Reading, deleting, responding* • *Making your own messages* • *Finding specific e-mails*

The first half of the e-mail equation is reading mail, of course. Fortunately, you've already done most of the heavy lifting when you set up your e-mail accounts. Getting and reading your e-mail is a piece of cake on the iPad — similar, in fact, to how desktop e-mail programs work.

You can tell when you have unread e-mail by looking at the Mail app's icon. (It's usually in the Home screen's dock.) The cumulative number of unread messages appears in a little red circle in the upper-right area of the icon. You can also set new-mail alerts via the Notification Center pane in the Settings app.

TIP

You can check for new messages at any time by tapping the Refresh button (the circular arrow icon) at the bottom of the message list.

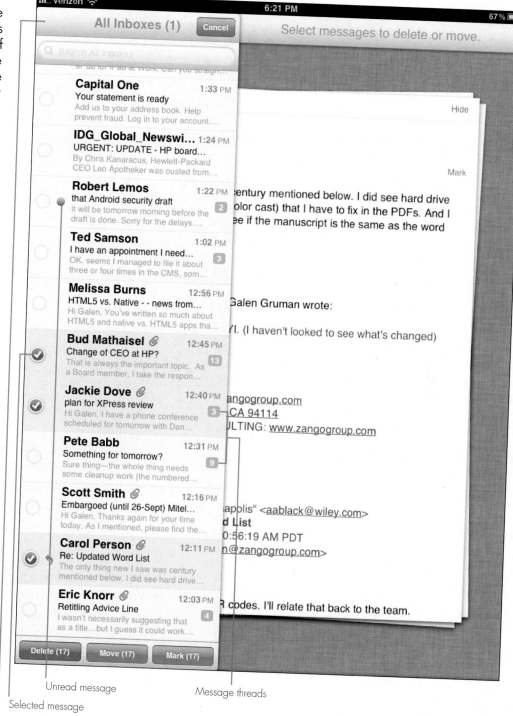

Unread message

Selected message

A mailbox or folder

Message threads

Reading

To read your e-mail, start by opening the Mail app. If you're holding the iPad in portrait position, tap the Inbox button to display the mail list if the contents aren't already displayed. In landscape orientation, the mail list is always visible. Note that the button's name changes based on where you are in your e-mail hierarchy: It can be Mailboxes, All Inboxes, Inbox, or the name of a folder or an account.

When you're reading a message on the screen, the buttons for managing incoming messages appear at the top of the screen. If you need to scroll to see the entire message, just place your finger on the screen and flick upward to scroll down.

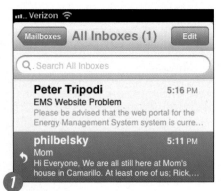

① If the e-mail mailbox you want to see isn't front and center, tap the Inbox, Mailboxes, or folder button in the upper-left corner to find the appropriate one. Or, tap All Inboxes to see new messages from all accounts.

② A number next to the account name indicates how many unread messages it has. No number means no unread messages. In an inbox or folder, the unread messages have a blue dot to the left of their subject line.

③ Tap a message in the mail list to read it.

Replying and Forwarding

When you receive a message and want to reply to it, open the message and then tap the Respond button, which looks like a curved arrow, at the upper-right corner of the screen. Then tap Reply, Reply All, or Forward as desired in the menu that appears. (The Reply All option appears only if more than one recipient was on the original e-mail.) You may also see a Save Images button if that message has image attachments; tapping that button saves the images in the Photos app. The option you tap acts as follows:

✔ **Reply** creates a blank e-mail message addressed to the sender of the original message. **Reply All** creates a blank e-mail message addressed to the sender and all other recipients of the original message; that is, anyone in the From, To, and Cc fields (but not to anyone blind-copied). In both cases, the subject is retained with the prefix *Re:* added. So if the original subject were *iPad Tips*, the reply's subject would be "*Re: iPad Tips.*" You can enter your reply message at the top of the e-mail.

✔ **Forward** creates an unaddressed e-mail message that contains the text of the original message. Add the e-mail addresses of the people you want to forward the message to and then enter your message at the top of the e-mail. In this case, rather than the prefix *Re:*, the prefix *Fwd:* precedes the subject, for example, *Fwd: iPad Tips.*

You can edit the subject line of a reply or a forwarded message or edit the body text of a forwarded message the same way you would edit any other text. You can also add and delete recipients. To send your reply or forwarded message, tap the Send button as usual.

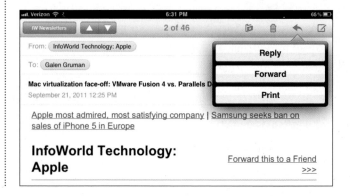

for DUMMIES

Marking and Flagging Messages

Often, when you read an e-mail message, you're not quite done with it. You want to mark it so you remember to look at it later. One method is to create a mail folder, as explained later in this section, and place mail messages in it — essentially, creating a tickler file for those messages you want to revisit.

But Mail provides two other, more visual ways:

- **Flag messages.** This adds a flag icon next to the e-mail in the message list and places a flag in the message's subject area when you view the message. (The flags are also visible in your computer's e-mail software.)

- **Mark messages as unread.** This adds a bullet icon next to the e-mail in the message list and places a bullet icon in the message's subject area when you view the message. (The messages also show up as unread in your computer's e-mail software.)

To mark a message either way (or both), you have these two options:

- **In the message itself:** Tap the Mark link and then choose the desired option — Flag or Mark as Unread — from the menu that appears. You can also remove the markers by choosing Unflag or Mark as Read, depending on the messages state.

- **In the message list:** Click the Edit button at the top, select the messages you want to mark

by tapping their circular check boxes, and then tap the Mark button at the bottom. You get the same Flag and Mark as Unread options as you do within a message itself (and the same Unflag and Mark as Read options for already marked messages).

If you delete a message and then want to view it again, go to Mailboxes and then tap the Trash folder. A list of deleted e-mails is displayed. If you want to retrieve one, just move it back into the inbox or mail folder by using the Move button (the folder icon).

Deleting

When you no longer want an e-mail cluttering up your inbox or message folders, you can delete it. You can use these three methods:

- To delete a single message from the inbox or a message folder, flick to the left or right on the message's subject line. The Delete button appears. Tap it to delete the message.

- To delete a single message while reading it, tap the Delete button (the trash can icon) at the top of the screen.

- To delete multiple messages at once from the inbox or a message folder, tap the Edit button at the top of the message list. Circular check boxes then display to the left of each message. Tap the check box for each message you want to delete; red check marks appear for each one selected. Then, tap the Delete button at the bottom of the message list.

Composing and Sending

The second half of working with e-mail is to compose and send messages. That's also easy to do on an iPad. To compose a new e-mail message in the Mail app, take these steps:

1 Tap the New Message button (the paper-with-pen icon). A dialog box appears for composing a new e-mail.

2 Type the names or e-mail addresses of the recipients in the To field; as you type, Mail looks through contacts and lets you select names from a menu. Tap the + button to the right of the To field to choose names from the Contacts app.

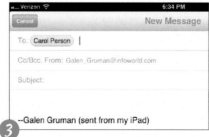

3 Fill in the Subject, type your message in the message area (immediately below the Subject field), and tap Send. Your message wings its way to recipients almost immediately if you're connected to the Internet.

Filling in the Subject field is optional, but it's considered poor form to send an e-mail message without one. Also, if you're not connected to the Internet when you tap Send, the message will be sent the next time you are connected.

More about sending mail

Mail looks up names in your Contacts app, any corporate directory in use (such as for an Exchange account), and people you've sent e-mail to previously. Although you can select groups from the Contacts app, the iPad doesn't let you create or edit groups; you must do that in your contacts application on your computer and then sync to the iPad to copy them to the Contacts app.

When you're sending an e-mail message, you can tap the field labeled Cc/Bcc, From. (*From* appears only if you have more than one e-mail account.) When you tap the field, Mail breaks it out into separate Cc, Bcc, and From fields. You enter recipients in the Cc and Bcc fields the same way as in the To field.

- **Cc** stands for *carbon copy,* and this field is used for people you want to see the message but aren't the primary recipients.

- **Bcc** stands for *blind carbon copy,* and this field is used for people you want to see the message secretly (so that no one else knows they got the message).

If you tap From, you can choose to send the message from any of your e-mail accounts on the fly, assuming, of course, that you have more than one account set up on the iPad. A list of accounts appears in a menu; tap the one you want to send this message from.

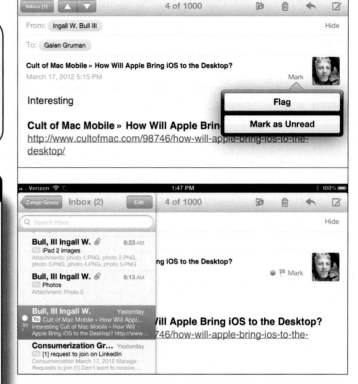

Flag or mark a message as unread when reading it using the Mark menu (top). The markers that result if both are applied (bottom).

Saving to Send Later

Sometimes you start an e-mail message but don't have time to finish it. When that happens, you can save it as a draft and finish it some other time. In the Mail app, compose your e-mail message, or at least some of it. When you're ready to save the message as a draft, tap the Cancel button in the upper-left corner of the screen. Tap the Save Draft button to save this message as a draft and complete it another time.

To work on the message again, go to the Drafts folder for the account you created the message in (your default account unless you selected a different From account before saving). A list of all messages you saved as drafts appears. Tap the draft you want to work on, and it reappears on the screen. When you're finished, tap Send to send it or tap Cancel to save it as a draft again.

Fancy Formatting for Your E-Mails

When you create e-mail messages on your computer, you typically have an option to apply boldface, indents, and other rich text formatting. The iPad has that ability, too. It's just less obvious how to use it because there are no formatting buttons onscreen.

DUMMIES

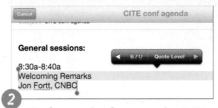

General sessions:
8:30a-8:40a
Welcoming Remarks
Jon Fortt, CNBC

1 Select the text to format. In the contextual menu that appears, tap the triangle icon to see the formatting options.

General sessions:
8:30a-8:40a
Welcoming Remarks
Jon Fortt, CNBC

2 To format the font, tap the **B**/U option. The three text-formatting options appear.

General sessions:
8:30a-8:40a
Welcoming Remarks
Jon Fortt, CNBC

3 Tap Bold, Italics and/or Underline as desired to apply the formatting. Tap outside the menu to close it.

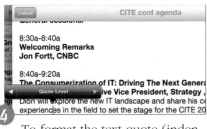

8:30a-8:40a
Welcoming Remarks
Jon Fortt, CNBC

8:40a-9:20a
The Consumerization of IT: Driving The Next Genera
ive Vice President, Strategy ,
Dion will explore the new IT landscape and share his c
experiences in the field to set the stage for the CITE 20

4 To format the text quote (indentation) level, repeat Step 1 but tap the Quote Level option instead of the **B**/U option. (If you have not selected at least one character, only the Quote Level option appears.)

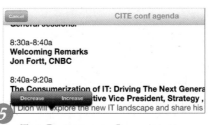

8:30a-8:40a
Welcoming Remarks
Jon Fortt, CNBC

8:40a-9:20a
The Consumerization of IT: Driving The Next Genera
ive Vice President, Strategy ,
Dion will explore the new IT landscape and share his

5 Tap Decrease or Increase as often as desired to reduce or add the quote indentation levels. Tap outside the menu to close it.

> **TIP**
>
> You can apply such formatting not just in Mail but also in Notes. If you're syncing notes to Microsoft Exchange, that rich text formatting is unavailable, so the contextual menus won't show formatting options when you select text. But you can format text for notes synced with other servers.

Searching E-Mail

If you're trying to find a message you sent or received, the iPad gives you two ways to do so:

- ✔ **In the Mail app,** go to the mail list for a specific inbox or folder and type your search term in the Search box at the top of the list. When you tap the Search box, four buttons appear below it. Tap the button you want to narrow your search to, for example:

  - The To button searches only names and e-mail addresses of people you've sent e-mail to.

  - The All button searches the From, To, and Subject fields plus (new in iOS 5) the message body.

  Tap the Search button on the onscreen keyboard to begin the search. Tap an e-mail in the results list to open it.

- ✔ **In the iPad's Spotlight app** (double-press the Home button or, from any Home screen, scroll to the left until it appears), enter a search

term in the Search box, and tap the Search button on the onscreen keyboard to begin the search. The results show any e-mails that include the term; tap an e-mail in the results list to open it.

To start a new search, tap the Delete button (the X-in-a-circle icon) in the upper-right corner of the onscreen keyboard to delete the term. Tap the Cancel button to close the search results and return to the mail list.

> **TIP**
>
> If you're using Exchange, iCloud, Gmail, MobileMe, or certain IMAP-type e-mail accounts, you may even be able to search messages that are stored out on the server, assuming you have an active Internet connection. When that option's available, you see the Continue Search on Server button in the search results.

Adventures in Mail Management

Your iPad's Mail app not only shuffles messages, but also gives you some of the more advanced options (just like your desktop e-mail program) that help you enjoy and manage your e-mail. For example, you can receive attachments; send photos, links, and documents to your e-mail recipients; and make use of the folder structures that you have in some existing mail accounts.

If you get an e-mail message with an attachment, chances are good that you can view that attachment and maybe even edit it or use it in another app. Sometimes a picture is worth a thousand words. When that's the case, you can use your iPad to send an e-mail message with a photo enclosed. You can view and use the folders from the e-mail client (such as Apple Mail or Microsoft Outlook) on your computer, but in iOS 5's Mail, you can create and delete folders directly on the iPad. Just be sure that you're working with your accounts, not your inboxes.

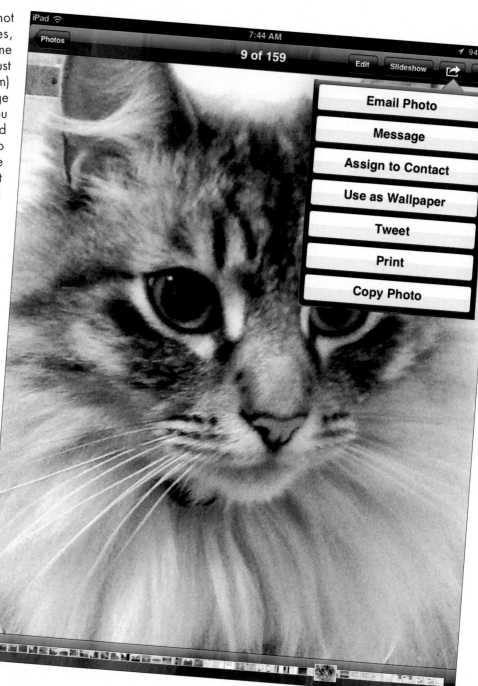

Sharing through E-Mail, Twitter, or iMessage

Sending a photo by e-mail on your iPad has a catch: You don't compose a message in Mail and then attach an image — the iPad doesn't work that way: Ditto for a tweet in Twitter and a text via Messages' iMessage service. Instead, you go to an app like Photos that has an image and send it from there.

This same technique works in all sorts of apps, including Safari (for sending web links); *The New York Times* and most other news apps (for sending links to stories); and office productivity apps such as Quickoffice, Documents to Go, and the iWork suite (for sending documents).

Here's an example with the Photos app:

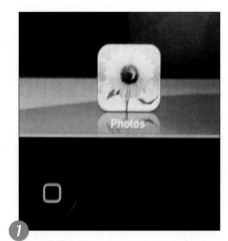

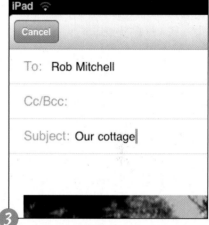

 On the Home screen, tap the Photos icon and find the photo you want to share.

② Tap the photo to select it and then tap the Share button. (It looks like a rectangle with a curved arrow springing out of it.) From the resulting choices, tap Email Photo, Tweet, or Message, depending on the way you want to share it.

③ Onscreen you see a message window with the photo already attached, embedded in the body of the message. Address the message and type any subject and text you want; then tap Send.

TIP

You can also click the Share icon button in the Photos app when an album is open; then tap the images you want to send (there's a limit of five for e-mails), tap the Share button, and then tap Email or Message. (You can't send multiple photos via Twitter.)

TIP

Different apps may have you select the attachments differently — Quickoffice, for example, has you drag them over a Mail button — but the fundamental process of starting in the app that has the files and sharing from there is true across the board.

Getting Attachments

Attachments appear at the bottom of the message as icons. Mail can display several types of attachments. GIF, JPEG, and TIFF images appear in the message itself; for the others, just tap the attachment icon to open it in the iPad's Quick Look capability.

In the case of large attachments, the iPad doesn't download the entire file until you tap it, so it's not wasting wireless bandwidth on attachments you don't intend to look at. You can tell if an attachment still needs to be downloaded because it'll have a big ⬇ icon on it.

Quick Look works with the following types of files:

- **Images:** GIF, JPEG, TIFF, and PDF.

- **Documents:** Microsoft Word, Excel, and PowerPoint; iWork Pages, Numbers, and Keynote; text-only (ASCII); and Rich Text Format (RTF).

- **Web pages:** HTML.

- **Contacts (VCF):** Tapping a VCF file adds the information to your Contacts app.

- **Calendar invitations (ICS):** Tapping an ICS file adds the appointment to Calendar.

To get back to your message from the Quick Look view, tap the Done button. If you don't see it, tap anywhere in the preview to display the onscreen controls.

If the attachment is a file format not supported by the iPad (for example, a Photoshop .psd file), you see the name of the file, but you can't open it on your iPad. If you have an app that can open it, read on.

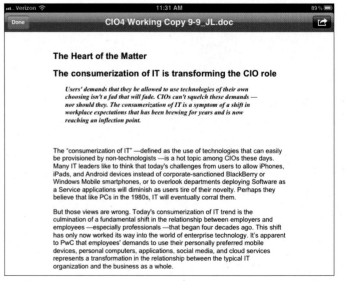

A document open in Quick Look

11:13 AM 92%

From: Julie Lynch — Hide

To: Terry Retter

Cc: Galen Gruman — Bernard "Bud" Mathaisel

Re: Approval Request for CIO Paper - The Consumerization of IT

September 14, 2011 3:59 PM — Mark

Hello,

The paper looks great. Thank you for inviting me to be a part of it. All my quotes are fine. I made one totally superfluous suggestion as a comment in blue - obviously feel free to take it or leave it.

Looking forward to hearing that it's published. Let me know if you need anything else.

- J

CIO4 Working Copy 9-9_JL.doc
863 KB

Julie Lynch
Principal, Uncommon Consulting

Attachments show up at the e-mail bottom.

The iPad has a capability called Open In that you can use with e-mail attachments (and files of all sorts in many apps). Open In lets you choose the application that you want to open the file in — if you have a compatible app. Using Open In is easy:

- ✔ Tap and hold the file attachment until a menu appears. (Note that if only Quick Look can open the file, no menu appears; instead, the file just opens in Quick Look.) If you tap Quick Look, the file opens in the Quick Look view. The menu lists other apps that can open the file; tap the app you want to use. You also see an Open In option, which if tapped provides a full list of compatible apps for you to choose from. (You may need to scroll within the pop-over to see all the options.)

- ✔ If you've opened the file in Quick Look and you have other apps that can open the file, you see an Open In button in the upper right of the onscreen controls. Tap the button to choose an app to open the file in.

Find another way to open an attachment.

Fiddling with Folders

If your e-mail account supports folders (as Exchange and IMAP accounts do), you can see these folders on the iPad — usually. If you tap an account in the Inbox list, rather than in the Accounts list, you don't see your folders, just messages in the inbox (the top-level folder). But if you're viewing an e-mail account, the Mail app on the iPad displays all folders that your e-mail account has. Tap a folder to open it.

To move e-mails into folders from the iPad, you have two options:

- ✔ **To move a single message** you're reading, tap the Folders button (it looks like a folder) at the upper right of the Mail screen. When the list of folders appears, tap the folder that you want to move the message into.

- ✔ **To move multiple messages** to another folder from the mail list, tap the Edit button at the top of the mail list. A circular check box appears to the left of each message. Tap the check boxes for the messages you want to move; red check marks appear for each one selected. Then tap the Move button at the bottom of the mail list and select the folder you want to move those messages to.

The iPad doesn't automatically sync mail folders; by default, it waits until you go to a folder to sync it. But, for Exchange accounts only, you can tell the iPad to update chosen folders automatically when it checks for new mail. Go to the Settings app and tap Mail, Contacts, Calendars. Tap the Exchange account with the folders you want to autosynchronize. In the resulting screen, tap Mail Folders to Push and then tap each folder to choose it.

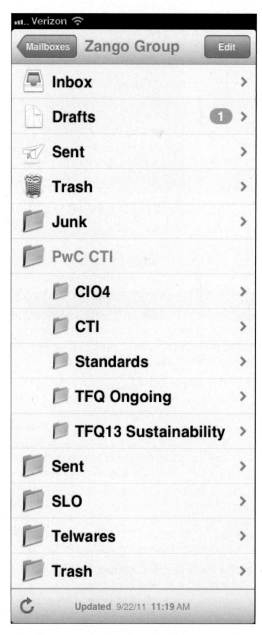

Tap a folder to see what's in it.

Before iOS 5, you couldn't create, rename, or delete folders on the iPad. But now you can.

The tricky part of the process is making sure you're working in an accounts list, not an inbox list. When you see the Mailboxes list, notice how it has two sections: Inboxes at the top and Accounts at the bottom. To edit folders, you need to tap an Exchange or IMAP account in the Accounts list.

Now it's easy. To add a folder, tap the Edit button at the top of the accounts list, which shows all current folders. Then tap the New Mailbox button that appears at the bottom of the list. (Mail calls folders *mailboxes.*) In the Edit Mailbox pane that appears, enter in a folder name and tap the account name under Mailbox Location to specify the folder

it should appear within (tap the account name to put it at the top folder level). Then tap Save.

To edit a folder, tap the Edit button at the top of the accounts list. Now swipe to the left over the folder you want to edit or delete. In the Edit Mailbox pane that appears, you can edit the name or change its mailbox location just as you would for a new folder. To delete the folder, tap the Delete Mailbox button.

Either way, click Save to close the Edit Mailbox pane and Done in the accounts list when you're done working on folders. When your iPad's Mail app syncs with your Exchange or IMAP server, the changes to your folders are made to the server and thus to all other devices that access that e-mail account.

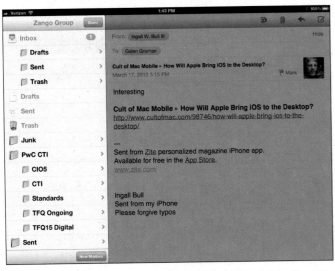

The accounts list needs to be visible to add or edit a folder.

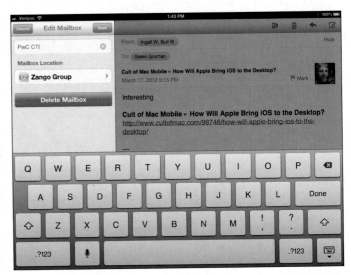

The Edit Mailbox pane where you specify a folder's name and location and, if the folder already exists, delete it

Customizing Mail

In the Settings app's Mail, Contacts, Calendars pane, you can find a lot of options for customizing how Mail works. There are three main groups of options:

✔ **Fetch New Data:** Tap this option to specify how often Mail checks for new messages. If the Push switch is set to On, Exchange and other push-compatible servers send new messages to you as you receive them. For POP and most free e-mail accounts, push isn't enabled, so you should set a time from the available options (every 15 minutes, every 30 minutes, every hour, or manually, which means when you tap the Sync button in Mail). If you have a mix of push and non-push e-mail accounts, be sure to set a time for those non-push accounts even if Push is set to On. You can give each account its own schedule by tapping the Advanced button.

✔ **The Mail section, group 1:** There are seven options in the first part of this section. *Show* lets you set how many old messages to load and keep available on the iPad for each account. *Preview* lets you set how many lines of each message to show in the message list.

Minimum Font Size lets you set the text size on messages. And the four switches let you control whether the To and CC labels appear in your messages' headers, whether you're prompted when deleting messages (to give you a chance to say no), load images embedded through hyperlinks in mail messages you receive, and organize messages by threads so all related messages are grouped.

✔ **The Mail section, group 2:** There's a grab bag of options in the second part of the Mail section. You can choose whether to always blind-copy yourself on messages you send, automatically increase the quote level in messages you reply to (so as the message bounces back and forth between replies, you can better track what was written when), specify the signature added to each new message (it's used for all accounts; you can't set separate ones), and specify the default account for new e-mails you create if you have multiple e-mail accounts (you can change this for each message before sending it).

Admiring Pictures

Photographs are meant to be seen, of course, not buried in the digital equivalent of a shoebox. The iPad affords you some neat ways to manipulate, view, and share your best photos.

The Fast Way

You've no doubt already figured out how to find a photo (hint: go to the Photos app) and view it full-screen and display picture controls (hint: tap the screen). But you can do a lot of maneuvering around your pictures without summoning those controls. Here are some options:

✓ **View the next or previous picture.** Flick your finger left or right.

✓ **Switch to landscape or portrait mode.** When you turn the iPad sideways, the picture automatically reorients from portrait to landscape mode. Pictures shot in landscape mode fill the screen when you rotate the iPad. Rotate the device back to portrait mode, and the picture readjusts accordingly. (The rotate lock must be off for this auto-rotation to work.)

Don't worry about which side is up on the iPad when you hand it to a friend to see a picture. The iPad always knows which is right side up.

The iPad adjusts a photo's display automatically based on the screen's orientation.

- **Zoom in or out.** Double-tap to zoom in on part of an image. Double-tap again to zoom out. (Or, use the expand and pinch gestures to zoom in and zoom out.) The downside to zooming is that you can't see the entire image.

- **Pan and scroll.** If you want to be the life of the party, after you zoom in on a picture, drag it around the screen with your finger. Besides impressing your friends, you can bring front and center the part of the image you most care about — for example, Fido's adorable face.

- **Skim pictures.** A bar appears at the bottom of the screen when you summon picture controls. Drag your finger across the bar in either direction to quickly view all the pictures in an open album.

- **Map it.** If you tap on the Places tab instead of an album or event, a map appears. Red pins on the map indicate that pictures were taken in the location shown on the map. Now tap a pin, and a stack of all the images on the iPad shot in that area appears.

You can spread your fingers on a map to enlarge it and narrow the pictures taken to a particular area, town, or even neighborhood.

Get Pictures from iTunes or Message

You can always transfer pictures from your computer to your iPad via iTunes. Connect your iPad and then click its name in the iTunes Sidebar. Go to the Photos pane and choose the source folder or, on the Mac, the iPhoto application, for the images to sync. If you use iCloud, the Photo Stream option syncs photos wirelessly between your computer (from the iPhoto or Aperture application or a specified folder) and the iPad's Photo Stream pane.

If an e-mail, a tweet, or a message has an image attached or you want to save a web page's image in Safari, tap and hold the image and then choose Save Photo from the menu that appears.

You can also get photos onto your iPad directly from a USB-equipped digital camera or from an SD card — if you have the Apple iPad Camera Connection Kit. The kit contains two adapters: the USB Camera Connector you use to import photos from a digital camera or iPhone, and the SD Card Reader to import from an SD card.

Get Pictures from a Camera or Card

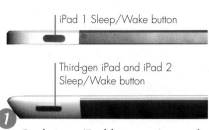

iPad 1 Sleep/Wake button

Third-gen iPad and iPad 2 Sleep/Wake button

1 Lock your iPad by pressing and letting go of the Sleep/Wake button on the top of the iPad.

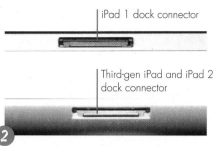

iPad 1 dock connector

Third-gen iPad and iPad 2 dock connector

2 Connect your USB Camera Connector or its SD Card Reader to the dock connector slot on the bottom of your iPad.

3 If you're using a camera, make sure the camera is on and set to transfer pictures; then connect the USB end of the cord that came with your digital camera into the USB Camera Connector. If you're using an SD card, insert it into the SD Card Reader.

REMEMBER

The Camera Connection Kit supports many common photo formats, including JPEG and RAW. The latter is a format favored by photo enthusiasts.

4 Unlock your iPad, and the Photos app on the iPad opens and displays the pictures available to import from the camera.

5 Tap Import All to select the entire bunch; to import individual pictures, tap them (a check mark appears next to each image you select) and then tap Import.

6 Disconnect the adapter — you're done!

Working with Albums

The Photos app organizes your pictures into albums. If you don't see the albums in Photos, tap the Albums tab at top.

The Photos album contains images you save from the web and from e-mail, as well as screenshots you take of your iPad screen. (To do so, press the Sleep/Wake and Home buttons at the same time.) The Last Import album stores images you most recently imported from your computer.

The Camera Roll album stores any photos or screenshots taken on the iPad. The Photo Stream album shows images synced across your computers and iOS devices through iCloud's Photo Stream syncing service; all photos in your Camera Roll album are automatically shared via Photo Stream. (Turn Photo Stream on or off in the Settings app's iCloud pane.)

Photos can appear in multiple albums because albums really are nothing more than groupings of photos for your convenience, not independent folders.

Other imported images are grouped in the same albums as they were on the computer, or lumped together as Events, Faces, and — when the embedded *metadata* inside an image by the camera identifies where a picture was shot — under a cool feature called Places.

There may also be albums for images you synced from devices such as your iPhone or digital camera. Here are the key actions you can take:

- ✔ **Tap an album to display its pictures.** You can also use the expand gesture to open an album. Using the expand gesture is handy because it lets you preview the image before opening it, and even rotate it so you can see it in its proper orientation. If you decide not to open an image you're previewing this way, just pinch your fingers before letting go.

- ✔ **Tap a picture to view it in full-screen size.** Or use the expand gesture to open a picture.

- ✔ **To go back to the album,** tap the button with the album's name or simply use the pinch gesture to close the image.

- ✔ **Scroll** up or down to see all the pictures in the album.

- ✔ **Tap an image to make the onscreen controls appear.** Tap it again to make them disappear; note that they disappear automatically after a few seconds if you don't use them.

Deleting Unwanted Pictures

Some pictures are meant to be seen. Others, well . . . you can't get rid of them fast enough. Fortunately, the iPad makes it a cinch to bury the evidence. Any pictures you synced to your iPad from your computer need to be deleted from the folder on your computer that you sync with the iPad (or moved to a folder that is not synced with the iPad) — unless you deleted it from the Photo Stream album, in which case all copies are deleted on other devices.

Then, the next time you sync via iTunes, the picture is removed from the iPad. But if the pictures came from the iPad — as a screenshot, as something saved from an e-mail, a website, or an app, or (except for the original iPad) from the built-in camera — you can delete them from the iPad. (The photos will reside in the All Photos or Camera Roll albums.) To delete a specific image:

1 Tap the picture you want to delete. Then tap the picture to get the onscreen controls if they aren't already visible.

2 Tap the Trash Can button and then tap the Delete Photo menu option that appears.

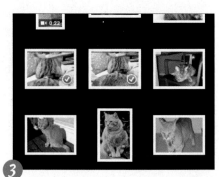

3 To delete multiple pictures: Go to the album holding them, tap the Action icon button, and tap each photo you want to get rid of; a check mark appears on each one. Verify the doomed bunch and tap Remove.

iPad Picture Tricks: Sharing and More

You can take advantage of the photos on the iPad in a few more ways. In each case, tap the picture and make sure that the picture controls are displayed. Then tap the Share icon button (the icon in the upper-right corner that looks like an arrow trying to escape from a rectangle). Doing so displays a photo-specific menu.

Here's what each menu option does:

- **Email Photo, Message,** and **Tweet:** Some photos are so precious that you just have to share them with family members and friends. When you tap Email Photo, the picture is automatically embedded in the body of an outgoing e-mail. Use the onscreen keyboard to enter the e-mail addresses, subject line, and any comments — you know, something profound, like "Isn't this a great-looking photo?" The Tweet option works the same for Twitter, and the Message option works the same for Messages.

- **Assign to Contact:** Assign a picture to someone in your Contacts list. To make it happen, tap Assign to Contact. Your list of contacts appears on the screen. Scroll up or down the list to find the person who matches the picture of the moment. Drag and resize the picture to get it just right. Then tap Set Photo.

- **Use as Wallpaper:** You may want to use a different image as the background, or wallpaper, for your iPad — a picture of your spouse, your kids, or your pet, perhaps? That's why the Photos app offers the Use as Wallpaper menu option. If you tap it, you see what the current image looks like as the iPad background picture. Move and resize the picture by dragging or pinching it. When you're satisfied with

the wallpaper preview, tap Set Home Screen to make it your new Home Screen wallpaper, Set Lock Screen to have the image appear when the iPad is locked, or Set Both for both.

- **Print:** Tap this menu option to print the photo to an AirPrint-compatible printer.

- **Copy Photo:** Tap this menu option when you want to copy a picture and paste it elsewhere. Alternatively, you can press and hold a picture until the Copy button appears. Tap that button, and now you can paste the image into an e-mail, for example, by preparing a message, tapping and holding until the contextual menu appears, and then tapping the Paste button to paste it into the body of the message. (You can also just tap and hold a photo until the contextual menu appears and tap Copy.)

TIP

iOS 5 lets you create new albums on the iPad. In the Photos app, go to the Albums pane, tap Edit, tap New Album, enter a name for the album, and tap Save. Then select the images you want to put in that album and tap Done. To add photos to an existing album, go to the album, tap the Share icon (the icon of an arrow emerging from a box), select the desired photos, tap Add To, choose either Add to Existing Album or Add to New Album, and then tap the desired album or give the new one a name.

TIP

You can also assign a photo to a contact by starting out in Contacts. From Contacts, choose the person, tap Edit, and then tap Add Photo. Select a picture from one of your iPad's albums. To change the picture you assigned to a person, tap the name in the Contacts list, tap Edit, and then tap the person's thumbnail picture, which also carries the label Edit. Select a new picture or delete the current one.

Showing Slideshows

- *Setting up slideshows and special effects*
- *Your iPad as a picture frame*

If you store a lot of photographs on your computer, you are familiar with running slideshows of those images. It's a breeze to replicate the experience on the iPad using the Photos app. You can even play music to accompany your slideshow. And when the iPad is locked, it can do something special: Turn into a handsome animated digital picture frame, which is a variation on the slideshow feature. If your iPad is not locked, press the Sleep/Wake button to lock it and put it to sleep. Then press either Home or Sleep/Wake to wake the iPad, which causes it to display the locked-iPad screen.

Here's how to set up a slideshow:

1 Open an album by tapping it in the Albums pane, or display all your photos in the Photos pane. You can have a specific photo open; if you do, the AirPlay icon button (a triangle-in-a-rectangle) may appear at the upper right.

2 Tap the Slideshow button in the upper-right corner of the screen. The Slideshow Options dialog box opens. To simply start the slideshow from here, don't worry about the options.

3 If you want to play music along with the slideshow, slide the Play Music switch to On. To choose the music that will play along with the slideshow, tap the Music field and, in the list that appears, tap any selection from your Music library.

4 Tap the Transitions field to get a list of effects and then tap the transition effect you want to use.

5 Tap the Start Slideshow button to play the slideshow. The slideshow ends when you press the Home button.

TIP

To run a slideshow that includes only the photos contained in a particular album, tap the Album tab, tap an album to open it, and then tap the Slideshow button to make settings and run a slideshow.

Set Playback Effects

Both the Settings app's Photos options and the Slideshow Options dialog box in the Photos app enable you to control the presentation of your slideshows. In the Settings app, you get extra capabilities: You can specify the length of time each slide is shown and display images in random order, as well as change the transition effects between pictures.

In the Settings app, tap Photos in the Sidebar and then tap any of the following options in the Photos pane:

- **Play Each Slide For:** The choices are 2, 3, 5, 10, and 20 Seconds.
- **Repeat:** If this option is turned on, the slide-show continues to loop until you stop it. If Off

is displayed, slide the control to turn on the Repeat function.

- **Shuffle:** Turning on this feature plays slides in random order. As with the Repeat feature, tap Off to turn on shuffle or tap On to turn off random playback.

When you're finished, tap the Photos button to return to the main Settings screen.

In the Photos app, you can set these same effects for the current slideshow. In the Slideshow Options dialog box, tap Transitions to get a list of available transition effects. Also, slide the Play Music switch and then tap the Music option to access your iPad's music library.

AirPlay Playback

There are two ways to send your slideshow to your TV if you have an Apple TV.

1. When viewing an individual photo or while the slide-show is playing, tap the image to make the controls visible, and then tap the AirPlay icon button and choose Apple TV from the menu before starting the slideshow.

2. After starting a slideshow from album view, double-press the Home button to open the multitasking dock, swipe to the left until you see the AirPlay icon, and then tap it and choose Apple TV from the menu.

Turning Your iPad into a Picture Frame

You can pause the slideshow by tapping the Picture Frame icon or sliding the Slide to Unlock slider to unlock the iPad. To disable the picture frame feature altogether, go to the Settings app, tap General in the Sidebar, then in the General pane tap Passcode Lock so that it's on (you'll have to enter your passcode at this point, if you have one), and slide the Picture Frame slider to Off.

To turn on the Picture Frame feature, tap the Picture Frame icon in the lower-right corner of the locked-iPad screen.

The Picture Frame icon

You can change how the iPad acts as a picture frame. Do so in the Settings app:

1 Tap Picture Frame in the Sidebar and then select the desired options from the Picture Frame pane on the right.

2 Set the transitions (dissolve or origami).

Turn the Zoom In on Faces feature on or off. Arrange to play slides in random or shuffle mode.

Choose between showing all photos or specific albums.

REMEMBER

You'd be hard-pressed to find a more appealing portable screen for viewing photos than the iPad's. So, in addition to the photo tricks that come ready to use on your iPad, I encourage you to check out the App Store. There you can find dozens of photography-related applications. These apps come from various sources and range from Photobucket for iPad (which is free), to the $0.99/£0.69 Photo Splash Effects, which lets you convert a picture to grayscale and leave a single object in the image with a splash of color, to the $2.99/£1.99 Photogene, which has photo-editing tools that help you straighten, sharpen, adjust color, and more.

TIP

To truly take advantage of the frame feature, prop up the iPad so that you can see it, such as by using a docking station, stand, cover, or case that can act as a stand.

Taking Pictures and Video

The third-gen iPad and iPad 2 let your tablet become your camera for taking still photos, shooting videos, and participating in video conferences — thanks to their front and rear cameras and the Camera and FaceTime apps that come preinstalled on it.

The third-gen iPad and iPad 2 come with two cameras, one in the front and one in the rear. They're basic: no flash, for example. The third-gen iPad's rear camera boasts 5-megapixel resolution and low-light enhancements for everyday use as an SLR or 1080p videocam, but the iPad 2's basic, 0.7-megapixel camera is suited just for web snapshots and 720p home videos. With the Camera app, you can switch between the front and rear cameras by tapping the button at the lower-right of the screen.

All photos are stored in the Photos app's Camera Roll album, which you can launch by tapping the button at the lower-left of the Camera app's screen. (It shows an icon of the last photo or screenshot taken.)

The Options button lets you turn the on-screen grid on or off (to help align your subjects properly).

Shooting Video and Making Movies

Shooting videos follows the same process as taking photos, except you use the slider at the lower right of the Camera app to switch to video-capture mode. Then tap the Record button to begin the video capture and tap it again to end the video shoot. (A timer appears on the upper right of the screen so you can see how long your video is.) Like photos, videos are stored in the Photos app's Camera Roll album.

The iPad's camera app is point-and-shoot simple

2. Tap the area of the image you want to focus on.

1. Switch between front and rear cameras.

3. Switch to video-capture mode here.

4. Tap here to take photo.

The real magic occurs when you take your raw video and make it into a movie. You can do that on your PC or Mac using video-editing software. Or you can do at least a basic job on the iPad itself using Apple's $4.99/£2.99 iMovie app, either as your final cut or as a rough cut that you work on from your computer after transferring the file from your iPad. iMovie lets you apply basic themes to a video, choose fade into options, and select music for the video.

2. Tap to start and end recording.

1. Choose the video-capture mode.

Click one of the following after using the retouch tools:

- **Save** (or **Apply** for the Red Eye tool or **Crop** for the Crop tool): Accept the change.

- **Undo:** Reverse the last change.

- **Cancel:** Undo all changes made by the current tool.

- **Revert to Original:** Undo all changes.

The retouching buttons in Photos (top) and a photo that is being cropped and slightly rotated within its mask (bottom)

Retouching Photos

The Photos app can do more than show and share images on your iPad: It can also do basic retouching of the photos you take from the Camera app or import through other means — as long as you have a third-gen iPad or an iPad 2, that is.

When you're viewing an image in Photos, tap the Edit button at the top to get the row of buttons at the bottom of the screen that you use to retouch the image:

- **Rotate:** Each time you tap this button, Photos rotates the image 90 degrees counterclockwise.

- **Enhance:** Tap this button to have Photos automatically adjust the color balance, brightness, and contrast to make the image look more vivid.

- **Red Eye:** Tap this button and then tap each person's eyes in the photo to remove the red-eye effect that often occurs when a photo is taken of people. (Tap an eye again to undo the red-eye removal.)

- **Crop:** Tap this button to get a grid you can use to align a photo by rotating its image with the grid as a guide or to crop the photo by dragging its sides to mask out the unwanted portion of the image. You can also expand or shrink, as well as move, the photo via gestures to change its focus relative to the grid. Tap the Constrain button to get preselected photo sizes such as 3 x 5 and 16 x 9.

Using iPhoto for iPad

The Photos app's built-in image enhancements take care of the basics, but they're no match for what you can do on your computer or what you can now do on the iPad. Although there have long been image-editing apps available for the iPad, such as Photogene and Snapseed, there are now two very powerful options (and surely more to come) that run on only the third-gen iPad and the iPad 2. One is Adobe's $9.99 Photoshop Touch, the iPad version of its Photoshop Elements application for both image retouching and creating original bitmap artwork. The other is aimed squarely at photo editing, and it's Apple's $4.99 iPad version of its popular iPhoto editor for Macs.

Although iPhoto for the iPad shares a name with iPhoto for the Mac, the iPad version isn't a clone of the Mac version but one designed from the ground up to work with the iPad's touch interface.

Any photos in the Photos app are available to iPhoto, and you access them through the familiar albums metaphor when you open iPhoto. After you select a photo, you can move to other photos in the same album by tapping one of their thumbnails on the side or the left- and right-arrow buttons on the bottom toolbar. Switch albums by tapping Albums. Tap Edit to enable the editing capabilities, which include the usual resizing via gestures, 90-degree rotation, cropping, and auto-enhancement controls at the bottom menu bar.

But that's just the tip of the iceberg. On the side of the menu bar (usually the left, but it can be the right) are the four sets of brushes:

iPhoto's Retouch brushes

✔ **Brightness and Contrast:** Not only can you adjust brightness and contrast with this slider (tap the lens icon), but you can also change the start and stop of the image's color range, the equivalent of changing the input curves in a program such as Photoshop.

✔ **Hue:** You get four sliders (tap the palette icon) to adjust the hue: one for overall saturation, one for blues, one for greens, and one for browns.

✔ **Retouch:** Pick any brush (tap the brushes icon) and then use your finger as a brush to apply its settings to whatever you brush on the image: Repair, Red Eye, Saturate, Desaturate, Lighten, Darken, Sharpen, and Soften. Tap the Settings button (the gear icon) to open a pop-over in which you can have iPhoto show onscreen where you've brushed the image so you can better control your strokes, as well as apply settings to the entire image, based on your current strokes.

✔ **Effects:** Tap the stars icon to get a set of color swatches that lets you tap a specific color effect such as Duotone or Vintage to colorize the image accordingly.

When you're done applying your effects, tap Edit again and then use the Share menu to save it to iPhoto or some external location such as iTunes or Facebook. There's more to iPhoto than I can describe here, but this should give you a strong starting point to take advantage of its amazing capabilities.

*iPhoto for the iPad . . . **is designed to work** from the ground up **with the iPad's touch interface***

The available controls for brushes (here, the Darken brush)

The Brightness and Contrast slider

The Effects swatches

FOR DUMMIES

Playing Your Tunes

N THIS ARTICLE

- *Listening to music and other audio*
- *Controlling the flow*
- *Adjusting volume and sound*

Y ou've heard of the iPod — a small, portable, music-playing device from Apple that's seemingly glued into the ears of many kids and teens. You probably use one, too. The iPad includes the Music app, which allows you to take advantage of the iPad's amazing little sound system to play your own style of music, podcasts, and audiobooks.

Your iPad is perhaps the best iPod ever. To use your iPad as an iPod, just tap the Music app's icon, which is on the right side of the dock at the bottom of the screen (unless you moved it elsewhere). Here's what you see in the interface when the Music app starts:

- ✔ **Content:** Most of the Music app is taken up by a grid of album covers you can scroll through to choose your desired music.

- ✔ **Library controls:** At the bottom of the window are buttons for changing libraries, such as to see what podcasts or playlists you have.

Controls
Rewind, Play/Pause, Fast-Forward, Repeat, Scrubber bar, Shuffle, Genius, Volume, AirPlay

Store

Libraries

Controls

Search

✔ **Player controls:** At the top of the screen, from left to right, you can see the Rewind/Previous Track button, Play/Pause button, and Fast-Forward/Next Track button on the left side, and the volume control and AirPlay on the right. In the center — but only if a song or podcast is playing — are the repeat control, the scrubber bar, the shuffle control, the Genius button, the name of the currently playing song

or episode, and an icon of the album or series it's from. At the bottom of the screen are buttons for the iTunes Store and the various libraries, as well as the search box.

✔ **Playlist controls:** The Playlist pane has one additional contol: the New button. Tap it, enter a name for the playlist, and then select the songs to add to that playlist.

Navigating the Libraries

At the bottom of the window are five buttons you tap to open these corresponding panes: Playlists, Songs, Artists, Albums, and More. (Tap More to get podcasts, genres, composers, and others' libraries shared over your network.) When you view certain libraries like Playlists, Songs, and Artists, you can see the letters of the alphabet running vertically (from A to Z) along the right side of the screen. When you're browsing through your tunes, tap any of the *quick-jump* letters to jump to items beginning with that letter instantly.

Also note the speaker icon that indicates the currently playing song or podcast.

Quick-jump letters

REMEMBER

If you're wondering about the difference between an artist and a composer, imagine this: You have a recording in your iTunes Library of a track entitled *Symphony No. 5 in C Minor*. The composer will always be Ludwig van Beethoven, but the artist could be the London Symphony Orchestra, the Los Angeles Philharmonic, or any of many other performers.

The Music app is your gateway to all your music, podcasts, and other audio files on your iPad. The figures on these two pages show the Albums pane (on the opposite page), a portion of the Songs pane (above), the Playtlists pane (at left), and Podcasts pane (below).

Working the Controls

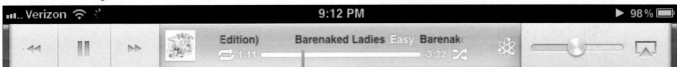

If you plan on using the Music app a lot, plan on getting familiar with using the controls. First things first: Tap a song or other audio file to play it. Then, use the following controls (located at the top of the screen) to manage playback:

- ✏ **Previous Track/Rewind button:** When a track is playing, tap once to go to the beginning of the track or tap twice to go to the start of the preceding track in the list. Touch and hold this button to rewind the track at double speed.

- ✏ **Play/Pause button:** Tap to play or pause the track.

- ✏ **Next Track/Fast-Forward button:** Tap to skip to the next track in the list. Touch and hold this button to fast-forward at double speed.

- ✏ **Repeat button:** Tap the loop icon to have the current song, podcast, album, or playlist repeat. (The icon turns black.) Tap again to have it repeat once. (A small numeral 1 appears on the icon.) Tap again to stop the repeat. (The icon turns white.)

- ✏ **Scrubber bar and playhead:** Drag the red line (the playhead) along the scrubber bar to skip to any point within the track. You can adjust the scrub rate by sliding your finger downward on the screen as you drag the playhead along the scrubber bar. The farther down you slide your finger, the slower the scrub rate. Neat!

- ✏ **Shuffle:** Tap the curved-X icon to have the Music app randomly play music from the current library (song list, album, and so on). Tap it again to stop shuffling. The icon turns black when shuffling is enabled and white when disabled.

- ✏ **Genius:** Tap the atom icon to create a playlist containing similar songs.

- ✏ **Volume control:** Drag the disc icon left or right to reduce or increase the volume level.

- ✏ **AirPlay:** Tap the triangle-in-a-rectangle icon to select a different output for the audio, such as an Apple TV or AirPlay-compatible speakers.

Full-Screen Mode

If you double-tap an album cover (or podcast, audiobook, or iTunes U equivalent) next to the Repeat control at the top of the screen when a song is playing, that cover replaces the Music app interface and displays in full-screen mode. Tap

Return to Library   Track list

the screen to have the iPad superimpose the audio controls, which you can then use.

But wait, there's more. Now, tap anywhere on the artwork that fills the screen and two additional controls appear at the bottom of the screen:

- ✏ **Return to Library:** Tap to go back to the Music app and the library you were viewing before you entered full-screen mode.

- ✏ **Track List:** Tap this button to see all the tracks on the album that contains the song currently playing. Tap any track to play it. Or, swipe across the dots above the track list to rate the song from one to five stars.

You can tap the album-cover screen again to hide the controls. Or when you're done, you can tap the Return to Library button at bottom left or any of the library buttons at the bottom center to return to the Music app's regular screen.

Volume and Equalizer Settings

You can tweak some settings to improve the sound performance of your iPad as iPod. Of course, there's volume control, but you also have equalizer settings that help you optimize the sound quality.

Change volume

1 With the Music app open, tap on a piece of music, a podcast, or an audiobook to play it.

2 In the controls that display, press and drag the disc icon on the volume slider to the right for more volume or to the left for less volume. You can also use the iPad's rocker switch or the volume controls in the multitasking bars if you're not in the Music app at the moment and don't want to switch to it.

Set max volume

1 Go to the Settings app and tap Music from the Sidebar to open the Music pane. Then tap Volume Limit.

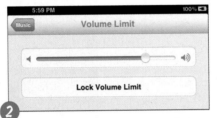

2 In the Volume Limit pane that appears, adjust the slider to the maximum desired level. Then tap Lock Volume Limit.

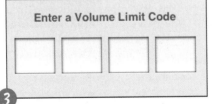

3 You're prompted to enter a 4-digit passcode, which someone must know in order to change this setting.

Stabilize volume

1 Go to the Settings app and tap Music from the Sidebar to open the Music pane.

2 Slide the Sound Check switch to On. The Music app will now adjust each song's volume to be the same as that of the other songs.

TIP

If you have the volume set at high and you're still having trouble hearing, consider getting a headset. Headsets cut out extraneous noises and may improve the sound quality of what you're listening to.

REMEMBER

Playing all songs at the same volume saves you from getting those surprise noise blasts or too-quiet songs, which can happen, for example, when shuffling.

Optimize sound

1 Go to the Settings app and tap Music from the Sidebar to open the Music pane.

2 Tap EQ to select a new equalizer setting to optimize frequencies for your music.

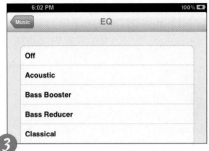

3 In the EQ pane that appears, select the desired equalizer; try out several while a song is playing to see which you prefer.

Sharing music

1 In the Settings app's Music pane, you can set the iPad to access your computer's iTunes music library — if home sharing has been set up on that computer and iTunes is running. Enter your Home Sharing ID and password in the Music pane.

2 In the Music app, tap the More button at the bottom of the window, tap Shared, and then select the desired library from the list of shared libraries found on the network.

Searching for songs and artists

You can find a particular song, artist, album, genre, or composer in several ways.

- With the Music app open, the easiest way to find music is to tap the Search box in the Music app and use the onscreen keyboard to type in a song, an artist, an album, or a composer name. Results display as you type.

- You can also find songs (or artists, for that matter) without opening the Music app by typing their names in a Spotlight search. (Go to the Home screen and flick to the left until the Spotlight Search box appears.)

Any-time controls

There's a quick-access trick for controlling your audio when you're using another application: Just double-click the Home button and swipe to the left to get to the playback controls shown below on the left.

When the iPad is locked, double-press the Home button to get the playback controls shown below on the right.

Exploiting Playlists

- *Making and playing playlists*   - *Letting a Genius choose your songs*

Playlists let you organize songs around a particular theme or mood: operatic arias, romantic ballads, British invasion — whatever. Older folks sometimes call them *mixes*.

Tap the Playlists button at the bottom of the window to see the available playlists, such as those synced from your computer's iTunes. And don't worry if you don't have any playlists. Just know that if you had some, you'd see them here.

Creating Playlists

You may find it easier to create playlists in iTunes on your computer, but your iPad makes it easy enough, as well, which the instructions on the next page show.

Listening to Playlists

1 Tap the New button at the top of the Playlist pane in the Music app, name the playlist, and tap Save.

2 You then see a list of the songs on your iPad in alphabetical order. (If you're playing an album or songs from a specific artist or genre, the list will be only for that selection.)

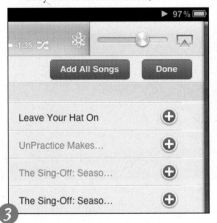

3 Tap the songs you want to have in this playlist; they turn gray. When you've tapped every song you want in the list, tap the Done button just below the volume slider.

To listen to a playlist, tap its name in your library to get a list of the songs it contains. If the list is longer than one screen, flick upward to scroll down. Tap a song in the list, and the song will play. When that song is over, the next song in the playlist will play. This continues until the last song in the playlist has played, at which point your iPad will shut up.

The iPad supports a special kind of playlist called the smart playlist. Although you can't create smart playlists on your iPad, they totally rock. What is a smart playlist? Glad you asked. It's a special playlist that selects tracks based on criteria you specify, such as artist name, date added, rating, genre, year, and many others. Fire up iTunes on your computer and choose File⇨New Smart Playlist to get started.

Calling on Genius

You can use the Genius feature in iTunes to set up playlists of recommended content in your iPad library. Based on items you've purchased, iTunes suggests other purchases that would go well with your collection. Okay, it's a way to get you to buy more music, but if you're building your music collection, it might be worth a try. To use the Genius feature on your iPad, you need to turn on Genius in iTunes on your computer and then sync your iPad at least once. On the iPad, if you tap the Genius button (the atom symbol) next to the scrub bar (you must be playing a song to see it), Genius tries to create a playlist composed of similar songs. In the Playlist pane, look for the playlist named Genius Playlist; open it to see Genius's 25 selections. If you like them, tap Save to save it under a name you specify. Otherwise, navigate to a different song and tap the Genius button to try again.

*… **turn on** iTunes **Genius** on your computer… **then** **sync** your iPad…*

When you tap a default Genius playlist (one that you did not create from a song), its first song begins playing; tap the Genius playlist to get a different song. (A Genius playlist does not show you a list of songs to choose from.) Genius playlists you created work like any other library, except they have a Refresh button that you tap to update the 25 Genius selections.

 The next time you sync your iPad, the Genius playlist appears in iTunes on your computer. Of course, you can also create a Genius playlist in iTunes on your computer and then sync it to your iPad.

Buying Music

● *Buying music via iTunes* ● *Getting music from other sources*

The iTunes app lets you use your iPad to download, buy, or rent just about anything you can download, buy, or rent with the iTunes application on your Mac or PC, including music, audiobooks, iTunes University classes, podcasts, and videos. And, if you're fortunate enough to have an iTunes gift card or gift certificate in hand, you can redeem it directly from your iPad.

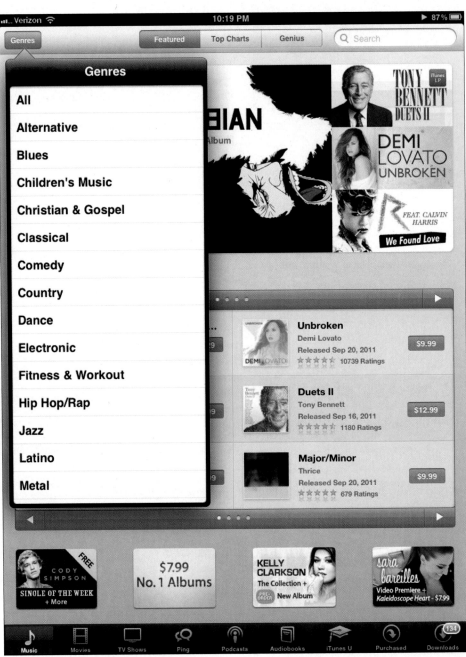

If you want to do any of that, however, you must first sign in to your iTunes Store account by tapping Store in the Sidebar of the Settings app. Then tap Sign In. If you don't have an iTunes Store account, tap Create New Account and follow the onscreen instructions.

After the iTunes Store knows who you are (and, more important, knows your credit card number), go to the iTunes app on your iPad and shop until you drop. It works almost exactly same as the iTunes App Store on your computer, where you can also shop — after all, wherever you buy the music, it all gets synced up. If you have a gift card, tap the Redeem button at the bottom of the iTunes app's screen to add its credit to your account *before* you buy something.

Explore the iTunes Store

Inside the iTunes app, you can explore what's available in the iTunes Store, as long as you have an active Wi-Fi or (for 3G or 4G models) cellular connection to the Internet. Tap the Music button in the row of buttons at the bottom of the screen, if it's not already selected. You can explore available music in several ways:

- ✔ **Tap the Next or Previous arrow** to scroll through Featured selections. Note that there are several sections in the Featured view, including New and Noteworthy and What's Hot, so be sure to scroll through the screen.

- ✔ **Tap the Top Charts tab** at the top of the screen. This displays two lists: one of top-selling songs and one of top-selling albums.

- ✔ **Tap the Genres button** to get a list of musical genres to narrow down the recommendations and available items.

- ✔ **Tap Genius** to get recommendations based on your previous iTunes Store purchases; note that you need to have enabled Genius in iTunes on your computer and synced with your iPad before this option works.

Checking Purchases

Tap the Purchases button at the bottom of the screen to see all the music you've bought at the iTunes Store. Tap the Not on This iPad button to see music you bought but don't have on the iPad. Tap an artist's name in the Sidebar to see the songs in the right pane, then tap the cloud icon to download all the songs or individual songs.

Remember that there's no charge to download music you've already bought to a device connected to the same Apple ID.

The navigation techniques in this list work essentially the same in any of the content categories (the buttons at the bottom of the screen), which include Music, Movies, TV Shows, Podcasts, Audiobooks, and iTunes U. Just tap on one to explore it.

If you want to buy music, you can open the description page for an album and buy individual songs rather than the entire album. When you find an item you want to buy, tap the button that shows either the price or the word *free*. The button label changes to Buy *X*, where *X* is the type of content you're buying. Tap the Buy *X* button. The iTunes Password dialog box appears; enter your password and tap OK. The item begins downloading and is automatically charged to your credit card. When the download finishes, you can view the content on your iPad using the Music or Videos app, as appropriate for the content.

Getting Music Elsewhere

The iPad, like the iPod, is very much tied to Apple's iTunes Store for purchasing music. But you can always import CDs into iTunes on your computer and then sync them to your iPad, as well as buy music on your computer in the MP3 format from online stores such as Amazon.com and then import them into iTunes for syncing with your iPad.

You can also use radio-like, subscription-based music apps such as Kazaa, Last.fm, Pandora, Rdio, Spotify, and Wunder Radio, though they require you to have an active Internet connection to access their millions of songs. Most such apps also let you create Genius-like playlists.

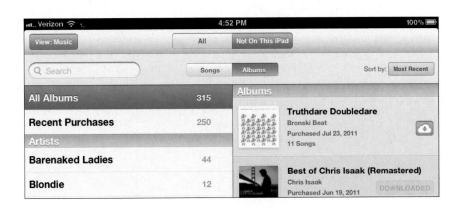

iTunes in the Cloud

A big change in iOS 5 is iCloud, the Internet-based service that stores and syncs files across your iPad and other devices. A big use for that is keeping your music, apps, and e-books available on all your iOS devices, as well as on your PC or Mac.

As noted on the previous page, you can download your iTunes purchases to the iPad, if they're not already synced to it. You can also tell the iPad to automatically download new purchases from the iTunes Store that you make on other devices. Just go to the Settings app, tap Store in the Sidebar, and then set automatic downloads to On for your choice of music, apps, and books. You can also have such automatic downloading happen when you're using your 3G or 4G account, though that will eat into your data allowance.

All that music can take up a lot of room on your iPad, though, so you might want to let Apple store it for you. That's what the iTunes Match service is for. The $25-per-year service removes the music from your iPad and keeps it online at Apple's servers until you want it.

When you use iTunes Match, you'll see an outline of a cloud next to all music in the Music app managed by the service. You play songs the usual way, but only after you download them from iTunes Match by tapping the download icon (the down arrow in a cloud) to get the desired music delivered to your iPad. This way, you store on the iPad only the music you're currently listening to. (To free up space on your iPad, just flick to the left over any song or album to delete it; it of course remains available in iCloud for later download.) But of course, you need a wireless or cellular connection to get to the music not yet downloaded.

iTunes Match stores not only the music you bought from iTunes but any music you've ripped from CD or bought in other online stores and imported into iTunes. You upload those files from your computer's iTunes when you turn on iTunes there. (Choose Store⇨Turn on iTunes Match.)

FOR DUMMIES

Podcasts, Audiobooks, and iTunes U

There's more to iTunes music than music. There's a whole world of *podcasts* — a form of Internet radio — and audiobooks in the iTunes Store, and there's a whole educational world of audio and video lectures available in Apple's iTunes U app.

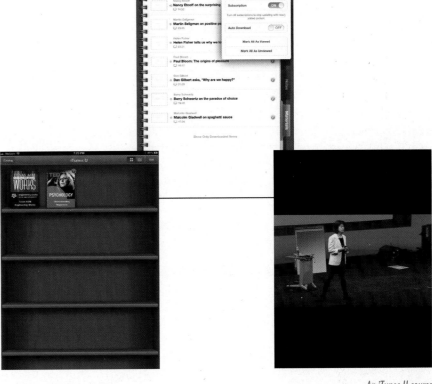

iTunes U: The World Is Your Oyster

Just where does that expression "the world is your oyster" come from, anyhow? I'm sure you can find out in iTunes U, Apple's app that lets to tap into a wealth of educational material.

Previously available as video and audio lectures in iTunes, iTunes U is now its own app that works very much like iBooks: You subscribe to a desired course or just download any of its individual lessons to the app's virtual shelves by tapping the Catalog button to open the iTunes U store at iTunes. If a course or lesson is a video, a rectangular quote bubble appears to the right of the title, along with the lesson's duration. If a lesson is an audio recording, you'll see just the duration in iTunes, but you'll see a speaker icon in the iTunes U app.

After you've downloaded a course, tap the course's binder on the virtual shelves to open its collection of resources. These courses are typically composed of video lectures that you download individually from the course binder. (They can be hundreds of megabytes, so getting the whole course all at once would take a very long time.)

Some courses have multiple sections. The course material itself is in the Materials section. (Tap the Materials tab to go there.) The Posts section shows instructions from the teacher to the students and can contain links to assignments and specific materials (videos, audio lectures, and textbooks) for

An iTunes U course

that lesson. The Notes section shows all the notes you've made in any e-books (distributed via iBooks) in the course material, as well as any overall notes you added directly in this section. Even better, these notes are synced to all your iOS devices connected to your iTunes account, so you can switch between your iPad and iPhone to go through a course.

REMEMBER

Accredited educational organizations can create their own coursework from videos, audio recordings, e-books, and iBooks Author textbooks, which they then assemble through their browser using an Apple web tool. To become a course provider for iTunes U, visit **https://eduapp.apple.com**.

Podcasts: Radio When You Want It

A *podcast* is simply a radio-style show distributed over the Internet. The concept has been around since the Internet, but it didn't take off until Apple's iPod, for which bloggers began creating audio downloads and making them subscribable through RSS feeds. Apple provided a mechanism in iTunes to manage those subscriptions and add them to the iPod's player, which migrated into the iPhone and the iPad.

Today, you can get thousands and thousands of podcasts (mostly free) via iTunes, from versions of professional radio programs and TV shows (podcasts can be audio-only or video) to the mad mutterings of a guy in his garage. You can also get podcasts at websites, which play in the Safari browser, but then you lose the ability to subscribe and ensure you don't miss an episode.

Downloading a podcast is easy: In iTunes, tap the Podcasts button to peruse the available podcasts, and tap the graphic or name of one that interests you. In the tile that opens, you'll see a list of available episodes; tap the button that shows its price or the word *Free* to download a specific episode.

Subscribing to a podcast is more effort: You have to go to iTunes on your computer, go to the iTunes Store, find the podcast, and click its Subscribe button. That ensures you get each future episode and that the episodes are synced with your iPad via iTunes syncing (through a cable or Wi-Fi). But note that iCloud doesn't sync podcasts for you, and they're not available via iTunes Match, either.

Regardless of however the podcasts are loaded into the iPad's Music app, tap the More button at the bottom of the app and choose Podcasts from the dialog box. You'll see your podcasts organized by "show"; tap the desired show to get a list of available episodes, and then tap the episode to play it. The playback controls are the same as for music with a few exceptions: The Share button lets you e-mail a link to the episode, the Speed button lets you change the speed (tap once for 2X, again for ½X, and again for 1X), and the Jump Back button lets you go back 30 seconds in case your mind wandered while listening. There are no repeat or shuffle controls, as there are for music.

Audiobooks: Read without Your Eyes

An *audiobook* is what you used to call a *book on tape* — a recording of the book's text so you can read, so to speak, while you're driving, running, exercising, or otherwise not able to deal with text. You buy these too in the iTunes Store, in the Audiobooks section. Like podcasts, you need to tap the Other button to be able to select Audiobooks and see the books you've purchased. You play them as you do podcasts; the controls are the same, in fact.

And, also like podcasts, iCloud doesn't keep audiobooks synced across your devices, nor are they accessible from iTunes Match — so be sure to sync them from iTunes if you want to, say, hear a book you bought on your iPad when you're at the gym with your iPod.

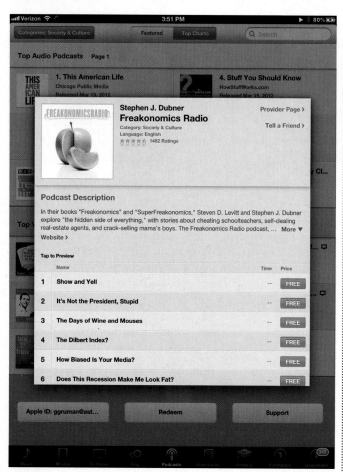

Download a podcast from iTunes on your iPad.

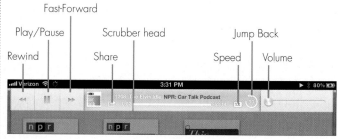

iTunes' playback controls for a podcast or an audiobook

Social Connections

E-mail was the first widely used communications tool on computers, and it's a big reason to use an iPad, too. But that method of staying in touch with friends and families is, well, so 1990s! Today, people socialize online in all sorts of venues: microblogging services such as Twitter, public status boards such as Facebook and Pinterest, professional communities such as LinkedIn, instant messaging, and video chat. The iPad is no stranger to any of these social tool and even has several of them baked in, including Twitter, instant messaging (via Apple's free iMessage service), and video chat (via FaceTime).

Keeping Up with the Tweeters

Twitter lets you keep your friends and other followers up to date on what you're up to, what you find interesting . . . pretty much anything you care to share in 140 characters or less. You can include hyperlinks to web pages and even attach images, and you can follow other people to have a constant stream of updates from people and companies whose tweets interest you.

The iPad's iOS 5 integrates Twitter, adding a Tweet menu option to the standard Share menu in Safari and other apps. Apps that don't use the standard Share icon button and its menu options often have their own equivalent button or control that typically also includes a Tweet menu option, and often buttons to share via other services such as Facebook and LinkedIn. And of course, many websites have such sharing buttons embedded in their pages.

But what makes the integrated Twitter on the iPad for the standard Share menu so nice is that once you provide your

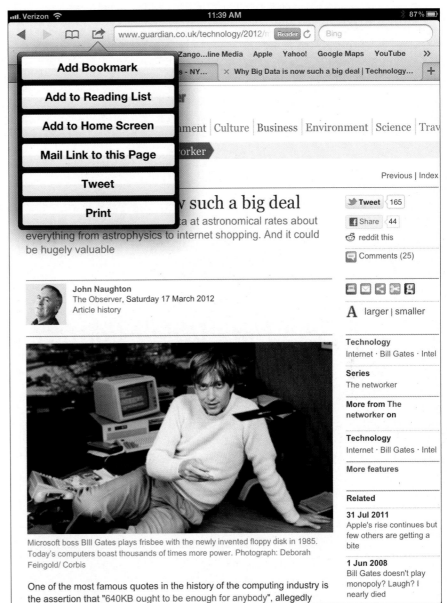

Microsoft boss BIll Gates plays frisbee with the newly invented floppy disk in 1985. Today's computers boast thousands of times more power. Photograph: Deborah Feingold/ Corbis

One of the most famous quotes in the history of the computing industry is the assertion that "640KB ought to be enough for anybody", allegedly

credentials to your Twitter accounts (yes, you can have several) in the Twitter pane of the Settings app, you don't have to sign in each time you tweet, as is often required when tweeting from websites. And those apps that use their own Share menu can also tap into your saved Twitter account information — if you allow it, of course; you'll be asked the first time an app wants access, and you can manage that access in the Twitter pane in Settings as well.

Manage your Twitter setup in the Settings app's Twitter pane.

You need to install the free Twitter app to use Twitter, even if just from the Share menu. A quick way to get it is go to the Twitter pane and tap Install. Or go to the App Store and search for it. You need the Twitter app to see the tweets you've sent and the ones from the people you're following.

The Twitter app

TIP

If you're a heavy tweeter and want to schedule tweets for future delivery, the free HootSuite app for the iPad makes it really easy. The big daddy of such enhanced Twitter services is, of course, TweetDeck, but it doesn't have a capable iPad app. So even if you use TweetDeck on your computer, you'll want HootSuite on your iPad.

Joining FaceTime Video Conferences

You can use the iPad's cameras to participate in video conferences using the FaceTime app that comes with the third-gen iPad and iPad 2, the iPhone 4 and 4S, 2010-edition and later iPod touch, and Mac OS X 10.6.5 Snow Leopard or later. *Note:* You have to connect via Wi-Fi to use FaceTime; you cannot use it on a 3G or 4G cellular connection.

The FaceTime app makes the process easy: Launch the app, choose a contact from the list at the right, and then tap the iPhone number or e-mail address. If FaceTime is enabled on that contact's device, he or she gets a badge indicating that you want to connect to the Internet via FaceTime. If your contact agrees to the conference, the contact's image appears onscreen. (Your image shows up in a small window near the upper right.)

During the FaceTime session, you can turn the audio on or off, end the conference, and switch the camera using the controls at the bottom of the FaceTime app. If you switch to another app by pressing the Home button, the FaceTime session remains active, but the other person no longer gets a live video feed from your iPad (until you switch back to the FaceTime app).

REMEMBER

You can get quick access to your FaceTime regulars by adding them to the Favorites list. To do so, tap the Favorites icon at the bottom of the FaceTime app, tap the + button at the top of the screen, and then choose the contacts to add to the Favorites list. You can then go straight to the Favorites list to conference one of those people.

Choose a contact and send an invitation to connect via FaceTime.

Facebook and other social services

There are many, many other social services you can use on your iPad, either via the Safari browser or via an app. However, of the most popular services, Facebook, LinkedIn, and Cold Brew Labs' Pinterest, have native iPad apps. Google+ has an iPhone app you can use on the iPad, but it's candidly awkward to use that way.

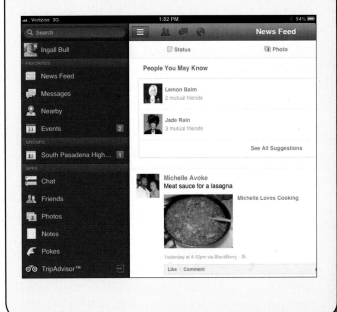

Using Messages

If you use an iPhone or other cellphone, you probably use its SMS messaging capability to send and receive quick notes. But the iPad, because it's not a phone, can't participate. Plus SMS messages cost either a fee per message or an added subscription fee on top of your smartphone service (such as for your iPhone). The Messages app and Apple's new iMessage service come to the rescue.

With iMessage, you can send and receive SMS-like messages with anyone else who has an iOS 5 device — iPad, iPhone, or iPod touch — from your iOS 5 device using the Messages app that used to be available on iPhones for just SMS messaging. (With iOS 5, iPhone users can use both SMS and iMessage in the Messages app.)

To use iMessage, go to the Settings app's Messages pane and select the e-mail accounts you want to use with iMessage. Other iMessage users can then select one of those e-mail addresses to send you iMessages. Macs will gain this capability when OS X Mountain Lion is released in summer 2012.

When you want to send someone an iMessage, enter their name in the To field, or tap the + icon to select them from your contacts list. If the person has an e-mail account associated with iMessage, the name gets a blue background; a

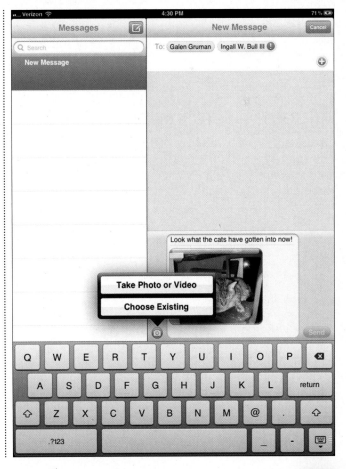

red background indicates the message can't be sent to that person (at least not via the e-mail addresses you have for that person).

Type a subject for your message in the Subject field and the message itself in the text field at the bottom of the screen. If you want, tap the camera icon to the left of the message screen to attach a photo or take a picture (if your device has a camera) to include. Tap Send when you're done — that's all there is to it. As you and the other person iMessage each other, you'll see the conversation unfold in the window.

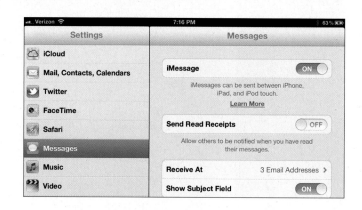

At the left of the message screen is a list of previous conversations with other people, so you can revisit them or even continue a previous conversation.

Keeping Up with Your Friends

You never know where a friend is; he or she could be just down the street or a world away. The free Find My Friends app from Apple lets you keep track of where your friends and family are and lets them keep track of your location, or at least your iPad's! (It also works on the iPhone, of course.)

With the Find My Friends app, if you haven't heard back from your sister-in-law in a few days, you might discover she's in Australia and probably on vacation, not ignoring you. You can tell when your husband is still at work and can probably stop by the store on the way home. Or that all your friends are at your house — no doubt a surprise birthday party is about to begin!

Of course, when you don't want your location known, you can tell Find My Friends to hide your location, and your friends have to give you permission to track them by responding to the invite you send from Find My Friends.

Find My Friends shows where your friends are.

TIP

If that little window showing your face covers up something you want to see during a FaceTime session, just drag it to any other corner on the screen.

DUMMIES

Contacts and Calendars

Staying in touch with people is a key activity in both business and personal contexts. So it should be no surprise the iPad includes the Contacts and Calendar apps to help you manage your address book and your appointments.

When you sync your iPad to your computer via iTunes or iCloud, you can sync contacts in the Mac's Address Book or Windows Address Book and calendars in the Mac's iCal, as well as contacts and calendars in Microsoft Outlook on Windows or the Mac, or in Microsoft Entourage on the Mac (with the proper settings).

TIP

If you use Microsoft Exchange (common for business e-mail, contacts, and calendars), iCloud, or Gmail, you can sync your contacts and calendars directly over the Internet as part of your e-mail setup.

TIP

In iOS 5, Contacts gives you four sharing options at the bottom of the person's card (scroll down to see them): Send Message (via the Messages app's iMessage service), FaceTime (for videoconferencing), Share Contact (e-mail or iMessage the details to someone else), and Add to Favorites (for FaceTime Contacts and the iPhone's Phone app).

However you sync, the iPad's Contacts and Calendars apps stay current, and any changes you make on the iPad are synced back to the address book and calendar on your computer or server.

The iPad wouldn't be all that useful for managing contacts if it just let you see what's on your computer's or server's address book. But it does much more, letting you add and edit contacts directly on the iPad as well.

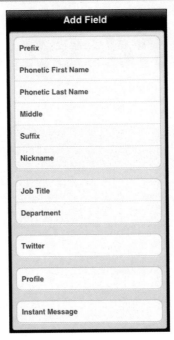

Adding fields (left) and editing contacts (right)

Add or Delete Contacts

To add contacts within the Contacts app, tap the Add button (the + icon) at the bottom of the screen and type in as much or as little profile information as you have for the person. Tap Add Photo to add a picture from your iPad's photo albums. Tap the other fields that you want to add information in. Note that two fields — Add New Address and Add Field — expand to offer more detail; tap the plus-in-a-circle icon to expand these fields. Use the Ringtone and Text Tone options to assign custom message tones. Tap Done when you're done entering the contact's information.

You can edit the information later by tapping the Edit button when a contact's name is highlighted.

To delete a contact, scroll down to the bottom of the contact information and tap the Delete Contact button.

Find Contacts

In the Contacts app, a list of your contacts appears in the left pane. Whatever contact is opened is displayed in the right pane, and the person's name is highlighted in blue in the left pane.

You have three ways to find a specific contact:

- Flick your finger so that the list of contacts scrolls up or down rapidly.
- Move your fingers along the alphabet on the left edge of the Contacts list or tap one of its tiny letters to jump to names that begin with that letter.
- Start to type the name of a contact in the Search box near the top of the Contacts list. Or, type the name of the place your contact works. When you're at or near the appropriate contact name, stop the scrolling by tapping the screen.

Then tap the contact's name to open it.

You can also change the way your contacts are displayed. In the Settings app, tap Mail, Contacts, Calendars in the Sidebar to open the Mail, Contacts, Calendars pane. Then scroll down to Contacts settings if it's not already visible. You have two options you can configure: Sort Order and Display Order. For each one, choose the First, Last option or Last, First to indicate whether you want to sort or display entries by a contact's first or last name.

Work with Groups

The one thing you can't do with contacts on the iPad is create groups. You have to manage groups on your computer or server, but you can add, edit, or delete the contacts within groups using the Contacts app.

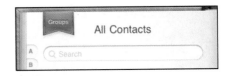

Tap the Groups ribbon icon at the top of the All Contacts pane. Any groups synced from your computer are listed first, followed by any groups available through a corporate Exchange server (if you're using one). To view or edit the contents of a group, tap that group to see its members in the left pane. Tap a member to get the full details in the right pane; it works just like individual contacts do.

If you use Exchange or other corporate server, you may see one of two special groups: Global Address Book or LDAP. That's the master address book for your company. You can search its contents the same way you would search for any contacts on the iPad, but you can't edit the contact entries it displays.

View and Navigate Calendars

The Calendar program lets you keep on top of your appointments and events (birthdays, anniversaries, and so on). The Calendar app's icon on the Home screen is smart: It changes daily to display the day of the week and date.

You have five main ways to peek at your calendars: the day, week, month, year, and list views. Choosing one is as simple as tapping the desired button — Day, Week, Month, Year, or List — at the top of the Calendar window.

The Calendar app's five views: Day (left), Week and Month (top row), and Year and List (bottom row)

If you use Microsoft Exchange or iCloud, you can add calendars from your iPad: Tap Edit, then tap Add Calendar. For other calendars, you have to create the calendars on your computer. (For Google calendars, you use the Google Calendar website.)

In each view, you have a slider at the bottom of the screen that lets you move through your calendar. In iOS 5, you can also just flick left or right to move through your calendar. In the Day view, you also get the current month's calendar, in which you can click any day to jump to it. In the List view, you can scroll up or down to previous or future dates. In all views, tap the Today button to jump to the current day's appointments.

Choosing Which Calendars Display

The iPad lets you display all of your calendars at once, using different colors to indicate different calendars, or you can see just specific calendars and hide the appointments from the others.

To pick the calendars you want to display, follow these steps:

① Tap the Calendars button at the upper-left corner of the screen. That summons the Show Calendars menu.

② Select each calendar you want to view by tapping its entry. A check mark appears next to that entry, indicating it will be displayed. Tap an entry again to hide the calendar; the check mark disappears. To show all the calendars, tap the Show All Calendars button. To make them disappear, tap the Hide All Calendars button.

③ Tap outside the menu to accept your changes.

Joining web meetings

A common way to hold meetings these days is via a web conference, so all attendees can see the same presentation or even each other.

The first-generation iPad doesn't have a camera, so you can't show yourself in a video conference. But you can still join one held via audio over the web by using an app for one of the major web conferencing services. With the later iPads, you can also join via video.

There are free apps for Cisco's WebEx, Citrix's GoToMeeting, and Fuze Box's Fuze Meeting web-conferencing services. Of course, you need accounts on those services to host the meetings from a computer (you can't host them from an iPad) and attend the meetings.

TIP

Use the Settings app to control Calendar's behavior. Go to its Mail, Contacts, Calendars pane and scroll down to the Calendars section. Here, you control how far back calendar entries are synced with the iPad, the default alert settings for appointments, the default calendar (if you use multiple calendars), and your home time zone (so when you travel your calendar stays in your specified time zone, if you also turn on the Time Zone Support option).

Adding Calendar Entries

Events in your life might range from business meetings to karaoke dates, but whatever the nature of your appointments, the Calendar app can help you keep them all straight. You can enter single events or repeating events and include alerts to remind you that they're coming up. It's easy to add events using iPad's Calendar app. Follow these steps and tap Done at the end to save the Event settings.

1 In any view, tap the Add button (the + icon) to add an event. The Add Event dialog box appears. In iOS 5, you can also just tap and hold where you want to add an event.

2 Enter a title for the event and, if you want, a location in the Title and Location fields, respectively. Tap the Starts/Ends field to enter the start and end times. The Start & End dialog box appears.

3 Flick your finger to scroll through the date, hour, minute, or AM/PM column and get the desired entry. You can also set the time zone if different than the current zone. Set each item and tap Done. (If the event will last all day, simply slide the All-Day switch to On and forget setting start and end times.)

4 To make an appointment a recurring one, tap Repeat. In the Repeat dialog box that appears, tap the desired option (in this case, Every Week) and tap Done to set it.

5 To have the iPad alert you (with sound and alert display) before an event begins, tap Alert. In the Event Alert dialog box that appears, choose how much advanced warning you want and then tap Done. You can set a second alert using the Second Alert option. (To specify the alert sound, go to the Settings app's General pane and then tap Sounds to set Calendar Alerts.)

6 To specify which calendar the appointment will be added to, tap Calendar and then choose the desired calendar from the list in the Calendar dialog box that appears. Tap Done.

Edit an Event

You can edit any event at any time by simply tapping it in any view of your calendar. The Edit Event dialog box appears, offering the same settings as the Add Event dialog box. Tap the Done button in this dialog box to save your changes. To delete a calendar entry altogether, tap the entry, tap Edit, and then tap the Delete Event button at the bottom of the Edit Event dialog box. You have a chance to confirm your choice by tapping either Delete Event or Cancel.

Handling Invitations

The iPad's Calendar app can send and receive meeting invitations through an e-mail server (Exchange or other compatible server). If New Invitation Alerts is turned on in the Settings app's Mail, Contacts, Calendars pane, the iPad intercepts any invitation sent to your e-mail, and the Invitations button label at the top of the Calendar app screen indicates the number of outstanding invitations. Tap the button to see invitation details and then tap a response (Maybe, Decline, or Accept). The sender sees your response, and if you tap Accept, you see the appointment in your calendar. If you tap Maybe, you see it in gray with a dashed outline. Sending invitations from a compatible account is also easy: When adding the event, you see an extra option in the Add Event dialog box:

*…the Invitations button **label** indicates **outstanding invitations***

Invitees. Tap it to open the Add Invitees dialog box. Type in your invitees' e-mail addresses or names from your contacts (in which case, the Calendar app adds the e-mail addresses for you). When you tap Done to save the appointment, an e-mail is sent to your invitees. Exchange users will see the invitation directly in their calendars. Non-Exchange users get an invitation attachment (an ICS file) that many e-mail programs can open and link to their calendars. To accept invitations via the Mail app (if you don't use Exchange), tap the invitation file attachment (the ICS file) at the bottom of the e-mail. Doing so adds it to your calendar. If you have multiple calendars, you get a pop-over from which you choose the calendar to add it to.)

Tap the Invitations button in Calendar to view calendar invites sent to Exchange and other compatible accounts.

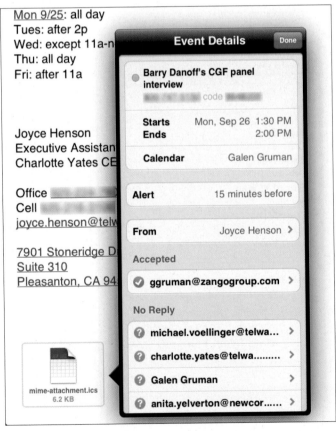

To accept invitations in other accounts, go to Mail and tap the ICS invitation file in the e-mail that contains the invite.

Taking Notes

IN THIS ARTICLE

● *Adding notes* ● *Working with notes*

The iPad comes with the Notes app to, as you'd expect, let you take notes. You can use Notes to do everything from jotting down notes at meetings to keeping to-do lists. It isn't like iWork Pages or Quickoffice by any means, but for taking notes and making lists on the fly, it's a great little app.

TIP

There's no need to save a note — it's automatically kept until you delete it.

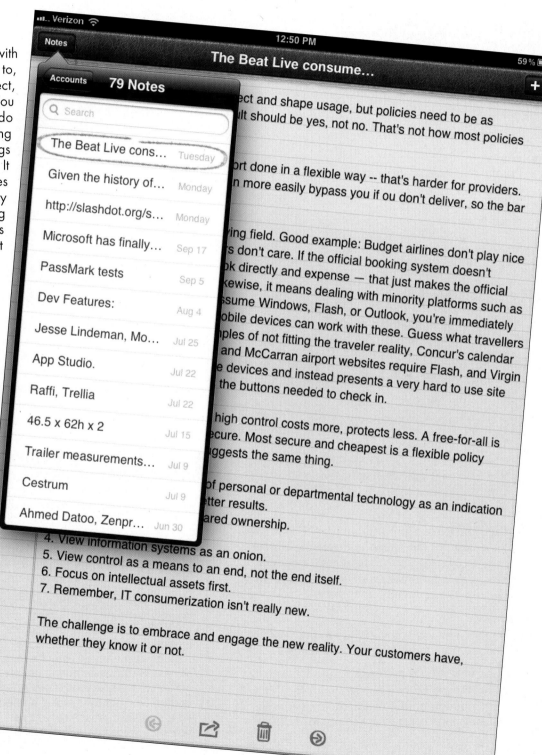

To create a note, follow these steps:

1 Open the Notes app.

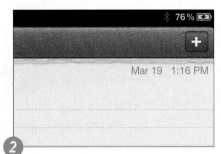

2 Tap the Add button (the + icon) in the upper-right corner to start a new note. The onscreen keyboard appears.

3 Just start typing on the blank note that appears.

When the Notes app is in landscape orientation, you can see a list of notes on the left side; tap any to move to that note. In portrait orientation, tap the Notes button to get a pop-over listing your notes; tap the one you want to go to.

You can also tap the ← and → buttons at the bottom of the Notes app to move backward or forward through your pile of notes.

Try these other functions of Notes:

- Tap the Share button (the icon of an arrow emerging from a rectangle) at the bottom of the screen to e-mail the current note using the Mail app or to print it (if you have an ePrint printer or a printing app).

- Tap the Delete button (the trash can icon) at the bottom of the screen to delete the current note. Delete any note in the notes list by swiping your finger to the left over it and then tapping the Delete button.

- Change the font for notes by going to the Settings app and tapping Notes in the Sidebar. Choose Noteworthy, Helvetica, or Marker Felt.

- To search your notes, enter text in the Search box at the top of the notes list and then tap the Search button on the onscreen keyboard. The resulting notes contain the text you searched for.

REMEMBER

Notes is a nice little application, but it's limited: It doesn't offer formatting tools, such as the ability to create bulleted lists or apply boldface. And you can't paste pictures into it — if you try, only the filename appears, not the image. So you may want to consider using a third-party note-taking app.

Syncing notes

Having the notes on your iPad can be handy, but if you're using a computer or an iPhone at the moment, those iPad notes suddenly aren't that handy. Fortunately, you can sync notes from your iPad to your computer and to the iPhone and iPod touch. In your computer's e-mail program, look for the option or preference that allows notes to appear in the Inbox.

You can also have notes sync via iCloud or via iTunes on your computer. For iCloud, turn the Notes switch on for each compatible account in the Settings app's Mail, Contacts, Calendars pane, as well as in your computer's iCloud system preference or control panel. To sync via iTunes instead, open iTunes on your computer and select your iPad in the Sidebar's Devices list. Go to the Info pane and be sure that Sync Notes is selected in the Other section. That way, each time you sync the iPad via iTunes, notes are synced as well.

Working with Reminders

iOS 5 brings to the iPad the Reminders app for managing to-do lists. Not only can you add and track tasks, but Reminders also integrates with iCloud, Microsoft Exchange, and IMAP e-mail servers, so any tasks accessible through those services are also available on your iPad. Plus any tasks added, modified, or deleted on your iPad are instantly updated to your computer and other mobile devices.

You specify which accounts Reminders works with in the Mail, Contacts, Calendars pane of the Settings app. Click an account, and if it's compatible with Reminders, you'll see a Reminders switch in the available controls. Move the Reminders switch to On to enable that account's tasks in Reminders. That's it!

The left pane of the Reminders app lets you switch among your task lists; tap an account to see its tasks. (You can't see a combined list from all accounts, unfortunately.) Tap List to see the tasks in list view, and tap Date to see the tasks in calendar view. Use the Search box to find specific tasks.

To add a new task, tap the Add (+) button at the upper right of the rightmost pane, then type in the text for that task. To mark a task completed, just tap the square to the right of its description; a check mark appears on completed tasks.

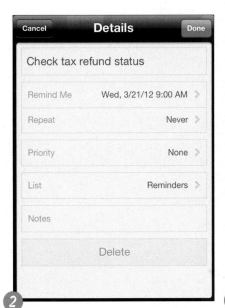

Tap and hold a task to open the Details dialog box, which you can use to set a reminder date and time for the task, make the task a repeating one, set its priority, specify which task list to move the task to, add notes, and delete the task.

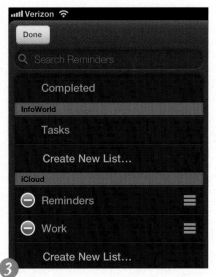

You can add new task lists by tapping Edit and then tapping Create New List in whatever account you want to add it in. Tap the icon of a white minus sign in a red circle to delete a task list, and drag the Rearrange icon (the three bars) to reorder task lists within an account.

The iPad and Files

● *Finding files*   ● *Printing documents*

The iPad is not just an entertainment device; it's a new type of computer that does many of the things that a Mac or Windows PC does. But it's not a Mac or PC and thus works differently in some regards — especially when it comes to working with documents.

Where Are My Files?

When you think of doing work, you think of using documents. Yet the iPad has no My Documents folder to store them in. It has no document folders at all, in fact.

The iPad can store documents, but it does so very differently than a computer. Document files are stored not in folders available to all the apps on the iPad but as part of the apps themselves. So the Photos app stores the photos in the app itself, for example. The same is true for the various productivity apps you might use on an iPad, such as the iWork suite or OmniGraph.

Before you exclaim, "Apple must be nuts!" there's a reason for this change. In a word, viruses. On PCs, files are stored in folders any app can access, and viruses and other malware take advantage of that to infect apps through the files they open. As a file is opened by other apps, they too can be infected. By getting rid of the common file system in the iPad's iOS, Apple ended that infection route.

The GoodReader app lets you mange files more like you can on a PC and then share them with other iPad apps.

So, to open a document, you first have to open the app that works with it. That's easy enough, but how do you get documents onto your iPad or off of it? Here's a refresher:

- ✓ **Sync files from iTunes.** In iTunes on your computer, select your iPad in the Sidebar's Devices list; then go to the Apps pane. You see a list of file-sharing-capable apps at the bottom. Click an app to get a list of files on the iPad; drag the desired ones onto your desktop or into a folder on your computer. To put files onto the iPad, drag them into the Sidebar's Library or onto the desired app in the Apps pane's File Sharing list and then sync your iPad.

- ✓ **E-mail the files.** In the iPad's Mail app, tap and hold a file attachment. In the menu that appears, choose the app you want to open it in or tap Open In to find additional apps that can open the file. Most apps have a send-via-e-mail feature (usually the envelope-style Share button) to send documents from the iPad.

- ✓ **Use a cloud storage service** such as Box, Dropbox, or SugarSync. Some apps can upload files to these Internet-based storage sites, as well as download files from them.

- ✓ **Use an "air-sharing" utility** such as the versatile GoodReader ($4.99/£2.99) to exchange files with your computer. These utilities require that your iPad and computer be on the same Wi-Fi network. They let you see your computer's files and then e-mail them or send them to a cloud-based storage service so you can then access the files on your iPad. GoodReader can also sync files via iCloud, via cloud storage services, via FTP servers, from websites, and even via e-mail servers. GoodReader has evolved way beyond air-sharing: It's a file manager in its own right, with its own folder system, plus the abilities to preview many common file formats and open zip files. And it provides full PDF markup capabilities. It's a must-have for working with files.

Marking up PDFs

When you open a PDF file in GoodReader, a toolbar appears at the left of the window. Tap a tool to display its options at the top of the window. Then tap the PDF to add a note, or drag your finger to highlight text, similar to what you would do on a computer.

You can work on the original or on a copy (you're asked which, when you first tap a tool), and GoodReader saves your changes as you work.

With these tools, you have all the major capabilities for PDF markup you'd expect on your computer using a tool such as Adobe Acrobat Pro on your iPad instead. And the annotations that GoodReader adds are fully compatible with Adobe Reader and Acrobat Pro, so you can share marked-up files with your colleagues easily.

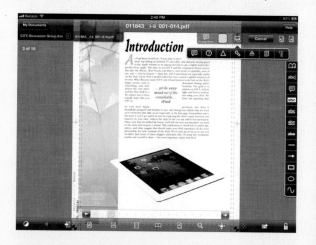

Sharing Files on the iPad Itself

When you have a file in an app on the iPad, how do you move it to other apps? Apple's mechanism for that is called Open In. Many apps that support Open In do so through the Share or other menu: Select a file, tap Share, tap Open In, and then choose the app in which to open a copy of the file. (The original is untouched, so beware having multiple versions.) Some apps, including Mail, let you tap and hold a file icon to open the menu of compatible applications to open the file in.

Some apps can work directly with Apple's Photos app to access copies of the images stored there, without needing to use the Open In menu. Likewise, the Cameras app can be accessed directly by other apps. iPhoto, GoodReader, and Snapseed have this direct connection, for example, which Apple has granted just to the Photos and Camera apps' content.

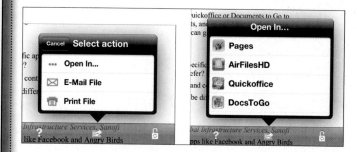

The Share menu with the Open In option (left) and the Open In menu with compatible apps for the selected file (right)

Productivity Apps

● *Using the iWork suite* ● *Glancing at Quickoffice and Documents to Go*

T he iPad is a great device for entertainment, web surfing, and keeping in touch with friends and family. But it's also very much a computer that can be used for work.

That's a good thing: In many cases, an iPad can be a lightweight, slim laptop replacement on short business trips. It fits in airplane's seatback compartments and tray tables, is unobtrusive on a train, and is easy to use in a waiting room. Plus the battery lasts 10 or more hours.

Don't take this to mean that you can chuck your laptop. Whether you use Windows or Mac OS X, the applications for those operating systems can do complex work that an iPad can't do (yet).

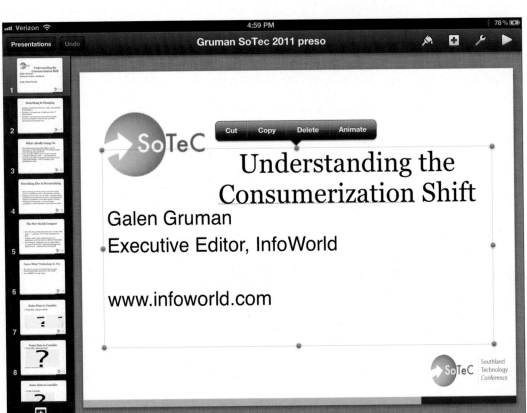

But the iPad is a great device for note-taking; for light word processing, slideshow, and spreadsheet use; for outlining and brainstorming; for reading of and commenting on work materials; for order-taking and other forms-based work; and more:

✔ Hospitals are adopting the iPad so nurses and doctors can look up and update patient records at bedside.

✔ Financial traders like the iPad as an information console to market data that they can then act on.

✔ Salespeople can check on customer orders and inventory levels and then place an order.

✔ Business execs can call up dashboards on performance meters.

For general-purpose productivity work — what you usually do in Microsoft Office — you have three options for the iPad: Apple's iWork suite (Pages, Numbers, and Keynote, which cost $9.99/£6.99 apiece), Quickoffice's $19.99/£13.99 Quickoffice Pro HD, and DataViz's $16.99/£11.99 Documents to Go Premium.

✔ Travelers can manage their travel arrangements, from confirming their check-in online to finding their way around an unfamiliar town.

Create an iWork Document

The iWork suite is a capable productivity suite available for iOS and Mac OS X.

Each iWork app — Pages, Numbers, and Keynote — has a similar look and feel, so even though they're separate apps,

knowing how to use one makes it easy to use the others. You create a new document in the same way for each of the iWork apps:

TIP

If you see Presentations (in Keynote), Spreadsheets (in Numbers), or Documents (in Pages) on the button in the top-left corner, you're not looking at the documents screen but instead, you're viewing an individual document; tapping that button takes you to the documents screen.

1 Launch an iWork app to see the documents screen.

2 Tap the Add New Document button (the + icon) at the upper left of the screen. Then tap Create Document (in Pages), Create Spreadsheet (in Numbers), or Create Presentation (in Keynote) in the pop-over that appears.

3 In the Choose as Template screen that appears, tap the template you want to use as a starting point, or tap Blank to start working with a completely empty document. Your new document opens on the screen.

REMEMBER

The iWork apps automatically save your changes as you make them. So if you switch to another app and come back, you'll find the document just as you left it.

Documents you can use

The iWork apps open native iWork files (Pages, Numbers, and Keynote) as well as their Microsoft Office counterpart files (Word, Excel, and PowerPoint). Pages also opens plain text files, and Numbers opens comma-separated text (CSV) files.

Sharing Documents

The iWork apps support the Open In interface, so you can open compatible files by tapping and holding their icons in Mail or other Open In-compatible apps and then choosing the appropriate app — such as Numbers, Pages, or Keynote — to open the file in from the Open In menu. For example, if you use a program such as GoodReader as a file-sharing app or maybe a cloud storage service such as Box or Dropbox for the same purposes, you can download a file into them and then use Open In to open the file in an iWork app.

To share documents from iWork apps, you have two options:

- ✔ Go to the documents screen and tap the Edit button at the upper right of the window. Then tap a file you want to share (you can share only one file at a time); the selected file has a yellow border around it. (Tap it again to deselect the file.) Then tap the Share button at the upper left and select the sharing method: Email, iWork. com, iTunes, iDisk, and WebDAV. WebDAV is a syncing technology that many online storage services support; for example, Dropbox users can pay $5 per month to get this capability (at **www.dropdav.com**), and Box users get it for free at **www.box.net/dav**. When you're done sharing, tap Done to return to the normal documents screen.

- ✔ If you're already working in a document, launch the Tools menu by tapping the wrench icon, choose Share and Print from the menu that appears, and then select the desired option from the submenu. The options are the same as from the document screen.

If you have an iCloud account, your iWork documents are automatically synced to all iOS devices connected to your iCloud account (assuming those devices also have the iWork apps installed, of course), as well as to your Macs using that same account (again if you have iWork installed). To sync documents via iCloud, be sure Documents & Data is turned on in the Settings app's iCloud pane, as well as in your Mac's iCloud system preference.

When iCloud is uploading the current version of a document from your iPad to iCloud for syncing with your other devices, an arrow icon appears in the document's upper-right corner. (iCloud also invisibly uploads changes to your document as you are working in it.) When iCloud is downloading document changes made elsewhere to sync with your local copy, a progress bar displays on the document thumbnail shown in the document screen.

You can also sync via iTunes on your computer, via the File Sharing section of the Apps pane for your iPad. Select the desired app, then drag files into its adjacent pane so they sync to your iPad. Drag out files in the pane to transfer them to your computer after syncing from your iPad.

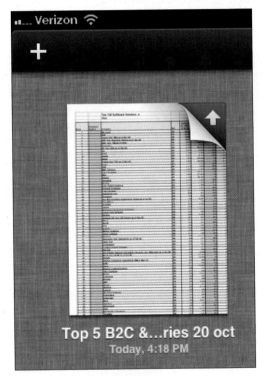

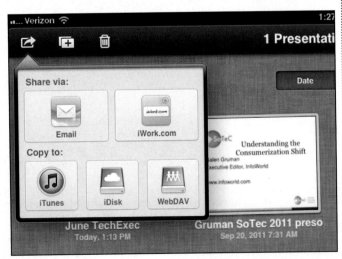

Sharing files from iWork apps

If multiple people are working on the same document simultaneously, or if somehow there are two out-of-sync copies of the document, you'll get a notice of the duplication when you open the document on your iPad. In that dialog box, you can choose which copies to keep.

Managing Documents

When you tap Edit in the document screen of an iWork app, two icon buttons appear in the upper left: Duplicate (the overlapping rectangles with the + symbol) and Delete (the trash can). Select one or more documents, then tap the desired button. When you're done duplicating and deleting, tap Done to return to the normal document screen.

Duplicate is a button you should get in the habit of using. When you open a document in an iWork app, there's no Save As option to save your changes separately from the original copy; every change you make is to the original. If you want to work on a copy, duplicate the file first and work on that copy.

To rename a document, tap the document name (not its thumbnail image) in the document screen. Then edit the name in the field that appears and tap Done when you're finished.

Edit a Document

When a document is open, a toolbar runs along the top of the screen. On the far-left side of the toolbar in Pages, the Documents button lets you see all your Pages documents. Numbers has the Spreadsheets button instead, and Keynote has the Presentations button. In all three apps, next to these buttons is the Undo button. At the right of the iWork toolbar are three common buttons in all the iWork apps.

- **Format (the paintbrush icon):** This button provides information and choices about the current selection in the document. For example, it lets you choose text color, text formats such as boldface, paragraph styles, text wrap, alignment, columns, and line spacing for selected text. If nothing is selected, this button is dimmed.

- **Insert (the + icon):** This button lets you insert images from the Photos app's photo albums. In some iWork apps, it lets you add other elements as well.

- **Tools (the wrench icon):** The button opens a menu containing tools that apply to the document as a whole rather than to the current selection in the document.

- **Play (the ▶ icon):** Available in Keynote only, this button lets you play your slideshow so you can see if the build effects work as expected and so you can practice your narration.

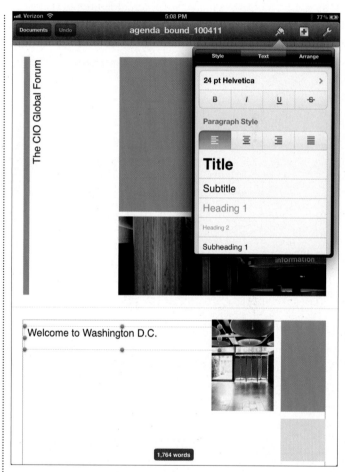

The onscreen controls when working on individual documents in Pages

When you import documents to work inside the iWork apps, they don't always come through clean. For example, fonts, headers, and bookmarks from the original document may be missing or altered. When that happens, the app displays a warning message.

Using Quickoffice Pro

A simpler alternative to iWork is Quickoffice Pro HD, which costs $19.99/£13.99 and can work with Word, Excel, and PowerPoint documents, as well as text-only documents.

For Word documents, Quickoffice can't place images in documents (though it retains any in imported documents), and it doesn't have dictionary lookup or the ability to copy and paste styles from one text selection to another, nor to apply styles to text at all. But its text formatting capabilities are similar, with the ability to set lists, indents and outdents, fonts, colors, and text size. And unlike Pages, Quickoffice doesn't wipe out the paragraph styles in your documents.

Quickoffice is more capable for Excel documents than it is for text documents. It works more like Excel than Numbers does, so you don't have to add tables to a sheet to be able to do anything. Instead, a new sheet has the standard rows and columns of Excel already available, so you can start adding data and formulas immediately. Quickoffice doesn't let you create charts in its spreadsheets.

For PowerPoint presentations, Quickoffice's tools are fairly sophisticated: You can add shapes, photos, and text boxes on any slide (including new ones), and you can add and edit text using formatting controls similar to those its word processor offers. You can also change the stacking order of a slide's elements. If you have the original iPad, Quickoffice lets you display your presentation on an external monitor, and when displaying from any iPad model, it has a neat additional feature where you tap on the iPad screen to display a laser-pointer-style highlight on the external screen. But Quickoffice has no slide notes or outlining capability.

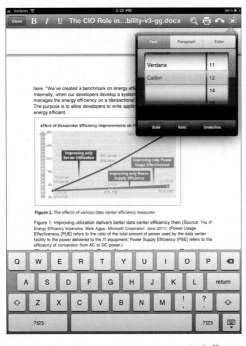

Quickoffice Pro

Documents to Go

Using Documents to Go

Another alternative to iWork is DataViz's $16.99/£11.99 Documents to Go Premium. It works with Word, Excel, and PowerPoint documents, as well as text-only documents.

For Word documents, DocsToGo (as the app is named on the iPad's icon and Open In menus) can't place images in documents (though it retains any in imported documents), has text formatting capabilities similar to those in Pages, and has a search-and-replace functionality. Unlike Pages, DocsToGo does not wipe out the paragraph styles in your documents.

If your spreadsheet contains a formula that DocsToGo does not support, you'll get a warning as it opens the file noting the cells and sheets affected. You won't be able to make any changes to that spreadsheet in DocsToGo. Also, note that DocsToGo appears to work only with a single worksheet; you'll see no worksheet tabs. But you can in fact work with multiple worksheets.

For presentations, DocsToGo has just basic capabilities. You can add notes to PowerPoint slideshows and edit (but not format) the text if you switch to outline mode. You can also delete slides and insert blank ones (placeholders for when you do the real work on your computer).

Cloud Storage

Cloud this, cloud that. You hear the "cloud" terms a lot these days. At its essence, it just means *online*, as in on the Internet. But whereas the Internet's usage has been mainly for delivering web pages, social networking, and online stores with digital goods (like the App Store), the cloud moniker suggests that nearly anything can be on the cloud. You can think of the cloud as a really big IT department someone else manages, and you just rent out the pieces you need. For most people, the part of the cloud that has the most immediate benefit is cloud storage, which is the ability to keep your files in one place and have them available on any Internet-connected device you own.

Dropbox and Box

Dozens of cloud storage services are available, but two are by far the most popular: Dropbox and Box. They work similarly on the iPad, with apps that let you transfer files to and from the iPad, view them on the iPad, and then open them in other iPad applications.

They also work on iPhones, Android smartphones, Windows PCs, Macs, and other devices, so you can access your files from almost anywhere you have an Internet connection — and even work on them if you have a compatible application on the device you're using. Both services let you e-mail files from the iPad as well, and both let you set up shared folders (you need to log in to their services via a browser to do this) so you can share files with others.

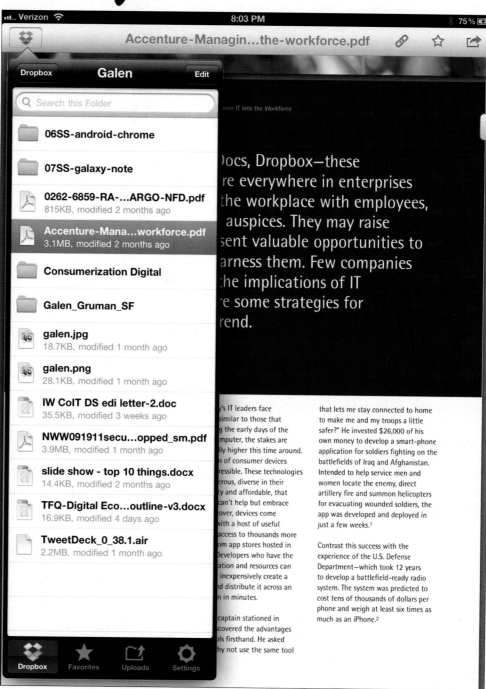

Dropbox

Dropbox is a bit easier to use because it lets you put a virtual hard disk on your Mac or PC to which you drag files to and from as you would any drive. Box requires you to upload files to and from your computer via your browser, which is extra work and just not that natural. But Box's iPad app does have a nice feature that lets you add comments to files it stores, so if you're sharing files with other Box users, you can trade comments.

Both apps are free, and both companies offer free basic service — so you can try them both or even use them both. Both charge monthly subscriptions to access more than 2GB of storage.

Accessing Cloud Files within Apps

Cloud storage apps are handy places to store lots of files, but using the Open In menu to copy them to other apps can be a real pain, plus it means you soon have modified copies of your files on the iPad and the originals stored on the cloud. Most apps' Open In menus won't let you put the modified files back in an app like Dropbox or Box, so you're really stuck.

That's why many cloud storage providers have provided mechanisms for programmers to access their storage servers directly from apps. Many apps integrate with Dropbox, Box, and Google Drive (formerly Google Docs), so you can open files directly within them. GoodReader, Quickoffice, and Documents to Go are three prime examples.

Making iWork Work with the Cloud

Notice I didn't mention iWork, Apple's productivity apps (Pages, Numbers, and Keynote), when naming apps that integrate with cloud storage services. They don't play as nice with others.

But they do provide a way to access some cloud storage services such as Dropbox and Box — through WebDAV, which is a standard for Internet-based file exchange. Your company could set up a Mac or Windows server to be a WebDAV server, acting as your own private cloud storage, for example. Well, Dropbox and Box have done just that.

To get files for use in iWork apps with any WebDAV-compatible server, click the + menu in the file list and then choose WebDAV. To save files to such a server, click Edit; in the Share menu that appears, choose WebDAV. You'll get a dialog box where you enter a URL for the DropDAV server, as well as your account name and password. Dropbox charges $5 for the service. (From an iWork app, enter **https://dav.dropdav.com**; to sign up, go to **www.dropdav. com**.) Box provides DropDAV support for free. (From an iWork app, enter **http://www.box.net/dav**.)

Many apps, such as Quickoffice, let you directly work with files stored on the cloud.

You may wonder why Google Drive isn't among my recommendations. The answer is simple: There's no Google Docs app for the iPad, so the only way to access a Google Docs file is via an app that can access it directly. (Working with files in Google Docs via the iPad's Safari can only be described as a form of cruel and unusual punishment.)

To access Dropbox and Box via an iWork app, sign in to their WebDAV services (as shown at top for Dropbox), and then navigate the folders as you would on a computer (at bottom for Box).

Using iCloud.com

You already know that iCloud syncs files, calendars, contacts, photos, bookmarks, and more among your iOS devices and Macs — and even many of these items with Windows PCs. But iCloud is also a website you can access from PCs and Macs (not from iOS devices) to upload and download files, manage your calendar, manage your iCloud e-mail account, manage your address book, and locate any iOS device or Mac for which Find My iPhone is enabled (covered later in this bookazine).

The Contacts, Calendar, and Mail features at iCloud.com work very much like the iPad versions of these apps and their Mac OS X counterparts, with just a few minor interface differences, but the iWork feature is a little special.

After you sign in to your account at iCloud.com and click the big iWork button, you get a web page with three panes, one each for Pages, Numbers, and Keynote. All the documents synced from these apps on your Mac and iOS devices are listed on their respective panes.

Click a document to download it to your current computer and then click the Download button that appears over it. You're then asked in what format to save the file (your choices are native iWork, its Microsoft Office equivalent, and PDF).

You can also upload files to iCloud, which is a handy way to add files that you can then access from iWork apps on any iCloud-enabled Mac, iPad, iPhone, or iPod touch. Click the Action icon (the gear icon) to get the menu whose options include Upload Document. (You can also duplicate, delete, and sort documents from this menu.)

The iCloud.com website

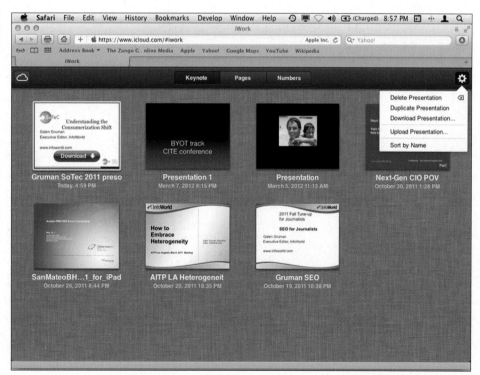

Working with iWork files on iCloud.com

Locating Anything

- *The Maps app's views*
- *Navigating maps*
- *Getting traffic status*
- *Searching locations*

1 f you own an iPhone, you'll find the Google Maps app on iPad to be very familiar. The big difference with iPad is its large screen, which lets you view all the beautiful map visuals plus new terrain and street views.

The Maps app has lots of great functions, serving as a showcase for the iPad's location-detection capabilities:

- Discover where you are and bookmark locations to return again.

- Get the phone numbers and web links to nearby businesses.

You can even look at a building or location as if you were standing in front of it, add a location to your Contacts list, or e-mail a location link to your buddy.

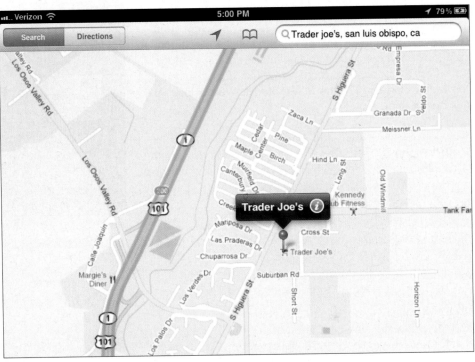

Classic view

Views, Zooms, and Pans

The Maps app has four views: Classic, Satellite, Hybrid, and Terrain. By default, the Maps app uses the Classic view the first time you open it. To change views, here's what you do:

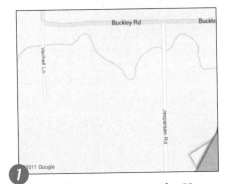

1 Tap the Maps icon on the Home screen to open the app. Swipe the bottom-right corner of the screen to turn the virtual page and reveal the Maps menu.

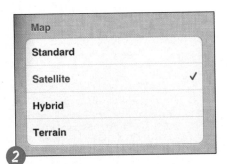

2 Tap the desired view option. In iOS 5, there's also the Print button for printing the current map to an AirPrint-compatible printer.

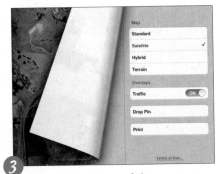

3 Flick the corner of the page to fold it back to view the map in the new view.

Whatever view you're using, you can zoom to see more or less of the map, or you can pan (scroll) to see what's above, below, or to the left or right of what's on the screen. Just use the standard pinch and expand gestures to zoom in and out and use the standard swipe gestures to pan. You can also double-tap the map with one finger to zoom in a fixed percentage, and double-tap with two fingers to zoom back out.

It can take a few moments for the map to redraw itself when you enlarge, reduce, or move around it, so have a little patience. Areas that are being redrawn will look like a blank grid, but will fill in over time. Also, if you're in Satellite view, zooming in may take some time because of all the image detail that has to be sent to your iPad. Wait it out: The blurred image will eventually resolve itself.

Satellite view

Hybrid view

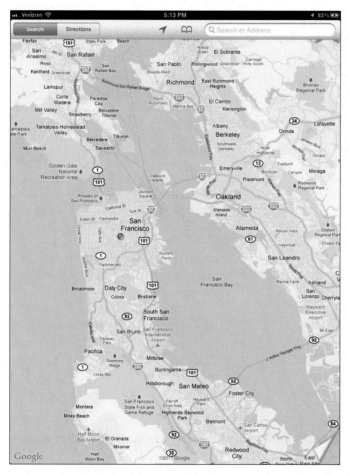

Reveal the Maps menu by swiping a map's lower-right page curl.

Terrain view

You can use the Maps app only when you're connected to the Internet via either Wi-Fi or (if you have a Wi-Fi/cellular iPad model) a 3G or 4G network.

Traffic Conditions

The Maps app also has a traffic overlay feature that you access from the Maps menu. If you live in a congested area, turn on this feature by sliding the Traffic switch to On. Maps then uses color highlighting on roads to indicate traffic speeds: Green means you're good to go, yellow indicates slowdowns, and red means avoid at all costs.

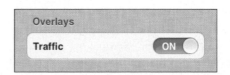

Traffic info doesn't work in every location, but the only way to find out is to give it a try. If no color codes appear on your map, assume that the traffic info doesn't work for that particular location. When you do see colors, they (officially) mean the following:

- ✔ **Green:** 50 or more miles per hour.
- ✔ **Yellow:** 25 to 50 miles per hour.
- ✔ **Red:** Under 25 miles per hour.
- ✔ **Gray:** No data available at this time.

Tracking Yourself

The iPad can figure out where you are at any point in time and display your current location. (Well, it can most of the time; if the iPad can't find a signal to a known Wi-Fi network or make a cellular connection, it won't know where you are.) After you open the Maps app, tap the Current Location button. (It looks like an arrowhead.) The icon turns blue, and a few seconds later, you see a blue circle that indicates your approximate location superimposed on a map. Double-tap the screen to zoom in on your location. If you move around, your iPad can update your location and adjust the map so that the location indicator stays in the middle of the screen — assuming you maintain an Internet connection while moving, of course. Realistically, to have the iPad follow you as you move any distance, you need to have a Wi-Fi/cellular model and have 3G or 4G enabled. But if you do, the iPad can let you know if you're following the Maps app's directions correctly by showing where you are continually.

Realistically, you need a **Wi-Fi/cellular iPad** *with* **3G** *or* **4G enabled**

Use ZIP codes in your searches to find nearby businesses. In the Search box, enter the ZIP code and then what you're looking for, such as **94114 pizza**, **57069 gas station**, or **90210 Starbucks**. Maps displays all locations matching your search term, each indicated by a pin. Tap a pin to get more details; tap elsewhere to close those details.

TIP

Maps controls

Current location, Bookmarks, Search box

For DUMMIES

How the iPad knows where you are

The Maps app uses iPad's location services capability to determine your approximate location using available information from your wireless data network.

Wi-Fi–only models use local Wi-Fi networks, whose locations are known thanks to the efforts of Google and others to map their locations throughout the world by driving through most towns' streets looking for Wi-Fi signals and recording each device's unique ID.

iPad Wi-Fi + 3G models use assisted GPS plus cellular data. Like many cell phones, the iPad has a GPS (Global Positioning Satellite) receiver that lets it communicate with satellites that can detect its location. It also communicates with nearby cell towers, which helps it calculate its relative location to them, assisting the GPS capability when needed.

Finding Landmarks

The iPad can also find locations pretty much anywhere in the world using the Search box in the Maps app. It works as you'd expect: Enter your search term and then tap Search. But you don't have to be so exact in your search terms. Enter what you know, such as **Eiffel Tower, Paris,** or **LGB airport** — the Maps app can often figure out what you're looking for. If not, it'll provide some suggestions. Do use commas to separate places and addresses from cities, and also use commas between cities and states, or cities and countries. You can enter postal codes at the beginning of a search term as well, not just at the end. In fact, in many countries, the postal code is entered before the city name, though you can enter it afterward if you prefer. The Maps app is flexible.

The Maps app automatically remembers locations you've searched for and directions you've viewed in its Recents pane of the Bookmarks dialog box. The Recents list appears when you tap in the Search box and start typing. To see this list if you're not searching, tap the Bookmarks button at the top of the Maps screen. If the Recents pane doesn't display, tap the Recents button at the bottom of the Bookmarks dialog box. To see a recent item on the map, tap the item's name.

Tap and hold the Current Location button to have it change to the Compass button. The map will then reorient itself to point north from your current location.

You can clear out all recent locations stored by Maps. Tap the Bookmarks button and then tap the Recents button. Tap the Clear button and then confirm by tapping Clear All Recents.

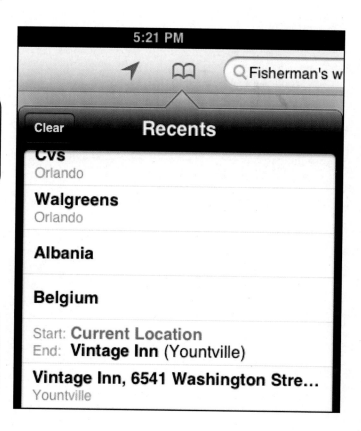

Bookmarking Locations

IN THIS ARTICLE

● *Dropping pins and bookmarks* ● *Using bookmarks*

1 n Maps, the bookmarking tools can save you from typing the same locations over and over again. You see these options on the Bookmarks dialog box that is displayed when you tap the Bookmarks icon to the left of the Search box. At the bottom of this dialog box are three buttons to switch among its three panes: Bookmarks, Recents (covered previously), and Contacts (covered later). You find out all about the Bookmark pane here.

TIP

The first things you should bookmark are your home and work addresses and your postal codes. These are things you use all the time with Maps, so you might as well bookmark them now to avoid typing them over and over.

Adding and Viewing Bookmarks

Bookmarks in the Maps app work like bookmarks in a web browser such as Safari. When you have a location you want to save as a bookmark to reuse later without typing a single character, follow these steps:

1. Swipe the bottom-right corner of your map view to turn the virtual page and reveal the Maps menu. Choose Drop Pin from the Maps menu.

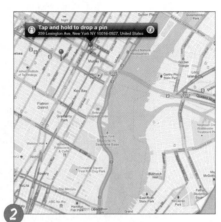

2. Drag the pin that appears to place it on the map at the location to bookmark. Tap the Information button (the *i* icon) to display the Info dialog box.

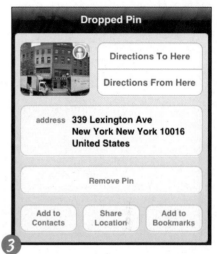

3. Tap the Add to Bookmarks button in the Info dialog box. The Add Bookmark dialog box and the onscreen keyboard appear. Rename the bookmark (if you want) and tap Save.

To view your bookmarks, tap the Bookmarks button (the open-book icon) located at the top of the Maps screen. If the bookmarks list isn't open in the dialog box that appears, tap the Bookmarks button at the bottom of the box. Then tap a bookmark to go to its location.

The Bookmarks dialog box before (left) and after (right) you tap Edit.

Managing Bookmarks

To manage your bookmarks, first open the Bookmarks dialog box by tapping the Bookmarks icon and then tapping the Bookmarks button if needed. Then tap the Edit button in the upper-left corner of the Bookmarks dialog box. You have two options:

- **To move a bookmark up or down in the Bookmarks list,** drag the Rearrange button (the icon with three gray bars) that appears to the right of the bookmark upward to move the bookmark higher in the list or downward to move the bookmark lower in the list.

- **To delete a bookmark from the Bookmarks list,** tap the Delete button (the icon of a minus sign in a red circle) to the left of the bookmark's name and then tap the red Delete button to confirm the bookmark's removal.

When you're finished using bookmarks, tap anywhere outside the dialog box to return to the map.

Locating Contacts

● *Finding a contact on the map* ● *Matching a location to a contact*

Maps and contacts go together like peanut butter and jelly. Here are some helpful tasks that illustrate maps and contacts at work together.

See a Contact's Location

To see a map of a contact's street address, take these steps:

1 Tap the Bookmarks button and tap the Contacts button at the bottom of the resulting Bookmarks dialog box.

2 Tap the contact whose address you want to see on the map.

TIP

If your search term matches names in your Contacts list, the matching contacts appear in a list below the Search box. Tap a name in the Suggestions list that appears to see a map of that contact's location. The Maps app is smart about it, too; it displays only the names of contacts whose entries have a street address.

Add a Location for a Contact

You can add any location to one of your contacts or create a new contact with a location you've found:

1 Tap the location's pin on the map and then tap the *i* icon to the right of the location's name or description to display its Info dialog box.

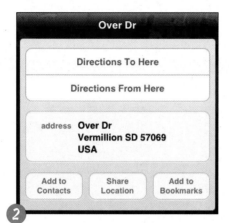

2 Tap Add to Contacts to begin creating a new entry in your contacts list or adding the location to an existing entry.

3 Tap Create New Contact or Add to Existing Contact. For a new contact, fill in the new contact information and tap Done. For an existing contact, just select the contact in the list that appears.

Location services beyond the Maps app

The iPad's location services help other apps besides Maps, of course. For example, the Urbanspoon and Zagat restaurant-finding apps use your current location to figure out nearby restaurants you might enjoy. The OpenTable app does the same to show you restaurants you can reserve online through its service. The Bank of America app is another that uses location information; in its case, to locate nearby branches and ATMs (as shown below). The Weather Channel app uses it to provide the local weather information wherever "local" happens to be at the moment. Transit apps (such as the iBART app for the San Francisco Bay area) use it to direct you to the nearest train station. You get the idea.

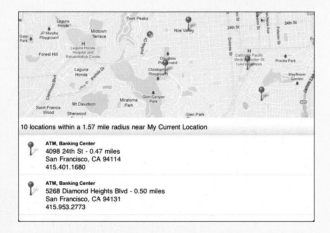

Note that you have to give an app permission to detect your location, so the first time an app needs that information, you get a prompt. You can enable or disable for each app whether it can detect your location in the Location Services pane of the Settings app.

Let the iPad Direct You

One of the Maps app's niftiest features is its ability to provide driving, transit, and walking directions. You start by specifying the start and end locations. When you've chosen both addresses, Maps displays the map with the directions highlighted as a route line. A blue bar also appears at the bottom of the screen, with estimated distance and travel time indicated.

REMEMBER

You can still change the Start and End fields after the route line and blue bar appear. When the start and end locations are correct, tap the Start button in the blue banner. Start changes to a pair of arrow buttons. Tap these buttons to display the next or previous step in your route.

Directions

Start field, Reverse, End field

Tap the Directions button to get the Start and End fields.

Choose the Start and End Locations

You have two ways to pick your start and end locations:

✔ **From a pinned location or current location already on the screen,** tap the pushpin and then tap the Information button (the *i* icon) to the right of the name or description to display the item's Info dialog box. Now tap either of the following options:

Directions to Here: Maps provides directions from your current location.

Directions from Here: Maps opens the Recents dialog box, from which you can select a location; you can also use the End field (a form of the Search box) above the Info dialog box to enter a location.

✔ **From any map screen,** tap the Directions button in the upper-left corner. The Search field transforms into the Start and End fields. Tap each field to open the Recents dialog box from which you can choose a location; or enter a search term in the fields to look for a different location.

Either way, you can swap the starting and ending locations by tapping the Reverse button (the stylized *S* icon) between the Start and End fields.

*Tap the **i** icon to open the Info dialog box.*

Using navigation apps

Although the step-by-step directions in the Maps app work well, the iPad doesn't offer the type of spoken turn-by-turn directions found on some GPS devices and apps. You know — where some friendly male or female voice barks out instructions such as "turn right on Main Street."

If you like those audible directions, you might want to get a navigation app such as CoPilot ($29.99/£24.99), TomTom ($49.99/£49.99), or Navigon ($59.99/£59.99). The other major navigation providers (Garmin and Magellan) didn't yet have iPad versions of their iPhone navigation apps available as of April 2012, but it's probably just a matter of time.

Get Directions Your Way

Using the Previous and Next buttons on the blue banner gives you step-by-step directions. If you prefer to see your driving directions displayed all together in a list, tap the List button on the blue banner; the directions appear in a dialog box. Tap any step in the list to see that leg of the trip displayed on the map. To scroll through the list, drag your finger up or down to determine the direction of the scroll. You can switch from the list to the one-at-a time directions by tapping the Restore button (the line-in-a-box icon) to the left of the word *Directions* in the dialog box. The list disappears, and the banner reappears with its arrow buttons.

TIP

When you're finished with the step-by-step directions, tap the Search button at the top of the screen to return to the regular map screen and the single Search box.

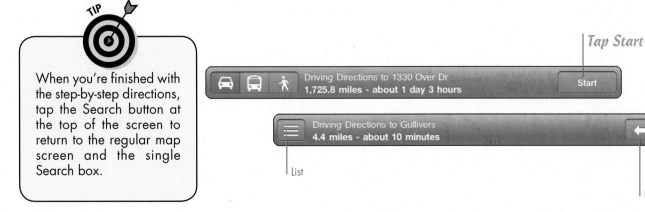

Tap Start

List

Next

Previous

Switch to Transit or Walking Directions

When you get directions in Maps, it shows you driving directions by default. But it can also display (in many areas, not all) transit and walking directions as well. To get these alternative directions, tap Transit (the bus icon) or Walking (the person icon) on the left side of the blue bar *before* you tap Start. There's also Driving (the car icon) if you want to go back to the driving directions.

If you tap the Transit button, the highlighted route changes on the map to match the recommended transit route. Also, the Timetables button (the clock icon) appears in the blue banner. Tap it to see the imminent departure and arrival times for the next bus or train. Tap the Depart button to enter in your intended departure date and time. If there are more travel options than can display, you can tap the Load More Times button to see additional departures and arrivals.

If you tap the Walking button, the highlighted route changes on the map to match the recommended walking route. Walking directions generally look a lot like driving directions, except for your travel time, of course.

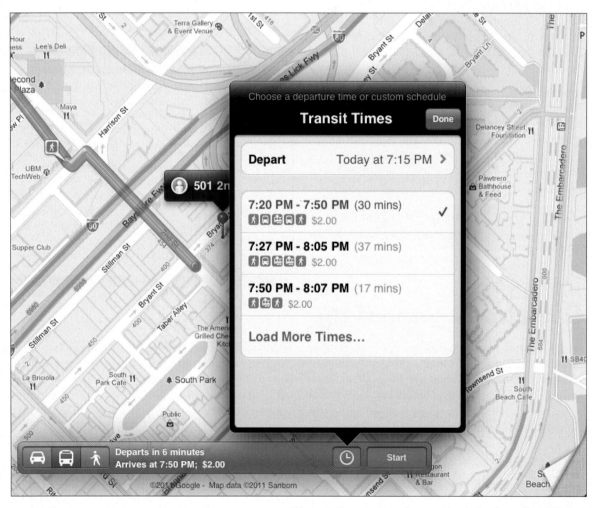

After you tap Start, you cannot change travel methods without redoing your search.

Protecting Your Location Privacy

It's great that your iPad knows where you are when you're seeking directions from point A to point B. And there's no way that apps such as restaurant finder Urbanspoon or price comparison-shopper Red Laser could help you find nearby businesses if they didn't know your location. Even the iPad's camera tracks your location so it can record metadata for the image about where you took photos and videos (as many digital cameras do). This feature helps you figure out later where you were shooting.

*The iPad lets **you** control who gets **your** location data…*

But it can feel creepy to know that your iPad is transmitting your location to others. Relax! The iPad lets you control who gets your location data and when. Whenever you first launch an app that uses your location information, you get a pop-up that asks for your permission to share it. And when an app is transmitting your current location, the location icon appears in the iPad's status bar. But what if you don't want an app always tracking your location, even if you gave permission? To control when your location is shared, you can turn permission on or off for each app in the Location Services pane in the Settings app. (Only apps that are location-aware are listed.) Just slide the control for each desired app to Off to disable location tracking and to On to re-enable it.

The status bar indicates when you are being tracked by showing the location status (arrowhead) icon.

Occasionally, you'll come across apps that track your location and don't seem to need to. Some of these may be spying on you, but chances are they have a location feature you're not aware of. For example, the Alarm Clock app tracks your location so it can present the current city name and weather in its clock. Other apps may use your location in ways you don't see the need for — such as when Quickoffice logs the location of created documents; in these cases, turn off the location tracking if it concerns you.

Alarm Clock displays your current city and its weather.

For each location-aware app, you can set whether it tracks your location.

Note: If you've turned off location tracking for an app and later use that app, it will ask again for permission to track your location. That way, you get a reminder so you don't inadvertently leave location tracking off when you do want it (such as when shooting a photo). When you're done, you can go back to the Settings app to disable tracking for that app.

Seeing Is Believing

Picture this scene: The smell of popcorn permeates the room as you and your family congregate to watch the latest Hollywood blockbuster. A motion picture soundtrack swells up. The images on the screen are stunning. And all eyes are fixed on the iPad.

Reality check! The iPad won't replace a wall-sized, high-definition television as the centerpiece of your home theater. But the iPad's gorgeous, nearly 10-inch, high-definition display — arguably the best screen on a handheld device — makes watching movies and other videos a cinematic delight. The screen looks terrific even when you're not viewing it straight on. And the third-gen iPad's Retina screen amps up the quality even more when you watch HD videos on it.

REMEMBER

In iTunes on your computer, you can choose which videos sync to your iPad by going to the Movies pane for your iPad (first select your iPad in the Sidebar's Devices list) and checking videos you want to sync to the iPad (or unchecking those you don't).

Apps to View By

Two of the applications that are included on your iPad focus on viewing video:

- ✔ **The Videos app** is a player with which you can watch downloaded movies or TV shows or media you've synced from your Mac or PC or downloaded via Wi-Fi via the iTunes app on the iPad.

- ✔ **The YouTube app** takes you online to the popular video-sharing site. YouTube videos range from professional music videos to clips from news or entertainment shows and personal videos of cats dancing and news-making events.

Fetching Stuff to Watch

You have a couple of main ways to find and watch videos on your iPad. You can fetch all sorts of fare from the iTunes Store, whose virtual doors you can open directly from the iPad's iTunes app. Or, you can sync content that already resides on your PC or Mac, from the iTunes Store there or from video you've imported into iTunes there. The videos you can watch via the iPad's Videos app generally fall into one of the categories shown in the table. (The free lecture videos that used to be available in the iTunes app are now available via the free iTunes U app instead.)

Source and Type	What You Do	Sample Prices
Movies, TV shows, music videos from the iTunes Store	Browse the iTunes Store's dedicated sections for purchasing episodes (or complete seasons) of TV shows (from *Glee* to *Modern Family*) and for buying or renting movies (from *Up in the Air* to *Avatar*).	$1.99/£1.19, single episode (standard def) $2.99/£2.49 single episode (high def) $34.99/£19.99, final season of *Lost* (standard def) $49.99/£24.99 final season of *Lost* (high def) $9.99/£5.99 to $19.99/£13.99, feature films
Rental movies from the iTunes Store	View rented films from their own Rented Movies section in the Videos app; there you see the number of days before your rental expires.	$2.99/£1.49 to $4.99/£3.49 (per 24-hour period)
Video podcasts in the iTunes Store	Watch, for example, free episodes that cover *Sesame Street* videos, sports programming, investing strategies, political shows, and so much more.	Just about all of them free!
Home movies or any previously downloaded video	Create a movie in iMovie or similar software on your Mac or PC. And enjoy all the other videos you've downloaded from the Internet or imported into iTunes.	Free or previously purchased

You have to completely download a movie onto your iPad before you can watch it — so you need to be on a Wi-Fi network or sync via your computer.

By tapping a movie listing in iTunes, you can usually watch a trailer before buying (or renting). Tap Preview and check out additional tidbits: plot summary, credits, reviews, and customer ratings, as well as other movies that appealed to buyers of this one. You can search films by genre or top charts (the ones other people are buying or renting), or you can rely on the Apple Genius feature for recommendations based on stuff you've already watched.

Playing Video

Videos stored on your iPad are segregated by category: Movies, Rented Movies, TV Shows, Podcasts, and Music Videos. Categories appear only if you have that type or source of content loaded on the iPad. When you decide what you want to watch, tap the Videos app's icon and follow these steps to watch it:

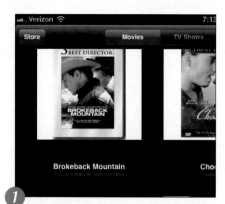

1 At the top of the screen, tap the tab that corresponds to the type of video you want to watch; its pane opens. Tap the poster image for a description and listing of cast and filmmakers.

2 Tap the Chapters tab to view the thumbnail images and chapter lengths. (For TV series, it's called Episode, and shows each episode you have.) Tap the Info tab to return to the description. (The two tabs are shown below.)

3 To start playing a movie (or resume playing from where you left off), tap the Play button (the triangle icon). From the Chapters pane, tap any chapter to start playing from that point.

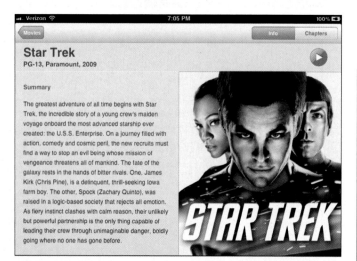

Changing the aspect ratio

Rotate your iPad to landscape mode to maximize a movie's display. If you hold the iPad in portrait mode, you can see black bars on top of and below the screen where the movie is playing. If the movie is widescreen (with a 16:9 aspect ratio), you get black bars above and below it in landscape mode.

You can double-tap the movie as it's playing to zoom in so the black bars disappear, though note the iPad will crop out part of the video on each side. Double-tap the movie again to return to widescreen view.

Controlling play

While a video is playing, tap the screen to display the controls. Then tap a control to activate it. Here's what each control does:

- ✔ **To play or pause the video,** tap the Play/Pause button.

- ✔ **To adjust the volume,** drag the volume slider to the right to raise the volume and to the left to lower it. Or use the iPad's physical Volume rocker switch to control the audio levels.

- ✔ **To restart or go back,** tap the Restart/Rewind button to restart the video or tap and hold the same button to rewind.

- ✔ **To skip forward,** tap and hold Fast-Forward to advance the video. Or, skip ahead by dragging the playhead along the scrubber bar.

- ✔ **To select language and subtitle settings,** tap the Audios and Subtitles button. You see options to select a different language, turn on or hide subtitles, and turn on or hide closed captioning. The control appears only if the movie supports any of these features and if you've turned on closed captioning in the Settings app's Video pane.

- ✔ **To tell your iPad you're done watching a video,** tap the Done button. The iPad displays the video's Info pane. Tap Movies (or Music Videos or whatever the video type is) to get back to the full list of available videos.

- ✔ **To make the controls go away,** tap the screen again (or wait a few seconds for them to go away on their own).

Video Controls

Audio and Subtitles, Rewind, Play/Pause, Fast-Forward, AirPlay, Volume

Deleting video

Video takes up space — lots of space. After the closing credits roll and you no longer want to keep a video on your iPad, here's what you need to know about deleting video from the Videos app and thus from your iPad's storage space (it's still in iTunes on your PC or Mac): To delete a video manually, tap and hold its movie poster until the small circled-X icon appears on the poster. To confirm your intention, tap the Delete button that appears or tap Cancel if you change your mind.

Will the video play on your iPad?

The iPad works with a whole bunch of video, but not everything you'll want to watch will make it through. Several Internet video standards — notably Adobe Flash — are not supported. The absence of Flash is a bugaboo for many folks, because Flash is the technology behind much of the video on the web today, though an increasing number of sites (for example, CNN, Reuters, *The New York Times*, *Time*, ESPN, NPR, the White House, and *National Geographic*) are offering iPad-compatible video in addition to the Flash format. What's more, entertainment apps from Netflix, Hulu.com, and ABC help fill the TV/movie void as well.

You may have to prepare imported videos so that they'll play on your iPad. To do so, highlight the video in question after it resides in your computer's iTunes library. Choose Advanced⇨Create iPad or Apple TV Version. Alas, this doesn't work for all the video content you download off the Internet or video you convert from your DVDs, including video files in the AVI, DivX, MKV, and Xvid formats. In these cases, you need help converting them to iPad-friendly formats using other software programs on your PC or Mac, such as HandBrake.

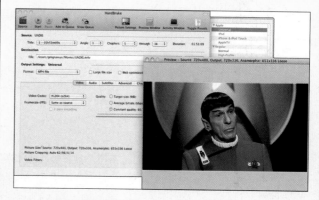

When the video is in a compatible format, you can import it into iTunes, where you can then sync it to your iPad.

If you delete a rented movie before you had a chance to watch or finish watching it on your iPad, it's gone. You have to pay to rent it again.

Watching YouTube

- *Finding and playing YouTube video*
- *Bookmarking, sharing, rating, and flagging*
- *Restricting video access*

Although you can go to YouTube and use all its features via the iPad's Safari browser, it's much easier to use the YouTube application that comes with the iPad.

Here's a quick tour:

- To see what other people like, tap your choice of the Featured, Top Rated, or Most Viewed buttons at the bottom of the screen. Note that the Top Rated and Most Viewed panes have buttons that let you specify the time period for the recommendations: Today, This Week, and All. You get a selection of videos.

- To find videos you'd like to watch based on keywords, tap in the Search field. The onscreen keyboard opens. Type a search term and tap the Search button on the keyboard. You get a selection of videos that match your search terms.

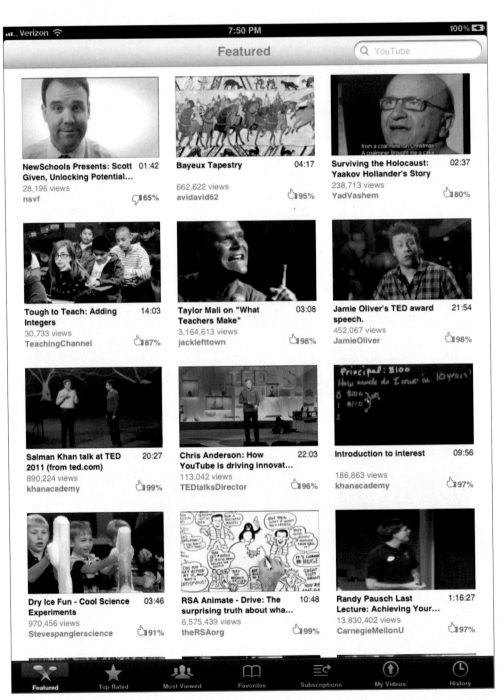

Tap to Play

✔ You can subscribe to videos, so if you like a video, you can get all future videos posted by the person who posted it. After you view a video and tap Done, tap the More From tab and then tap the Subscribe button to subscribe to all movies from this source. View your subscriptions by tapping the Subscriptions button at the bottom of the YouTube screen.

Note that you may get more results or recommendations than fit on a screen, so scroll down to see more videos. Tap any result that interests you to watch it.

TIP

When you stop watching a YouTube video (if in full-screen view, by tapping the video and then tapping Done), you can use the Related and More From tabs in the playback window to find additional content related to the topic or more videos posted on YouTube by the same source.

However you find your video, just tap it to play it in a window in the app. Of course, there's a little more to know:

✔ Tap the screen while the video is playing to get the onscreen controls. When the video is playing in the app window (as shown below), tap it to get the Play/Pause, scrubber bar to rewind or fast-forward to a specific point, AirPlay, and Full-Screen buttons. At top are the Add, Share, Like, Dislike, and Flag buttons.

✔ If you watch a video in full screen, tap it to get the controls below. From left to right: Bookmark, Rewind, Play/Pause, Fast-Forward, AirPlay, and Exit Full Screen.

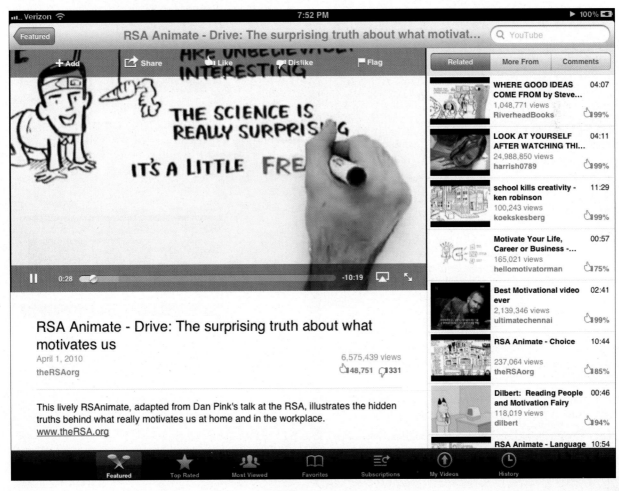

Adding a Video as a Favorite

Some YouTube videos are worth watching over and over again. But remembering their titles so you can find them in a search in the future is a hit-or-miss proposition. That's why you can bookmark your favorite videos by adding them to your Favorites list. How you add a favorite depends on how you're viewing the video.

Restricting video access

If you've given an iPad to your kid or someone who works for you, you may not want that person spending time watching movies or YouTube videos. Instead, you want him or her to do something more productive, such as homework or the quarterly budget. That's where parental (or boss) restrictions come in.

To restrict access to YouTube, start in the General pane of the Settings app. Tap Restrictions and, in the resulting Restrictions pane, tap Enable Restrictions. When prompted, enter and confirm a new or established passcode. In the YouTube row, slide the switch to Off instead of the default On.

When you return to the Home screen, the YouTube icon is missing in action. To restore YouTube, go back into Restrictions and tap Disable Restrictions or tap the Off switch so that it says On again. Of course, you have to reenter your passcode before you can do so.

Although you can't disable the Videos app completely, you can restrict movies or TV shows to certain categories, such as PG and below for movies and TV-14 and below for TV shows. In the Restrictions pane, tap Enable Restrictions.

- ✔ For movie restrictions, tap Movies and then tap the top maturity rating you want to permit.

- ✔ For TV restrictions, tap TV Shows and then tap the top maturity rating you want to permit.

1 If you're playing the video full-screen, tap the screen so the onscreen controls appear. Tap the Bookmark button (the book-like icon).

2 If you're playing the video in reduced view, tap the video so the onscreen controls appear. Tap the Add button.

3 To view your Favorites list, tap the Favorites button at the bottom of the YouTube screen.

Sharing, Rating, and Flagging Videos

YouTube gives you a voice with features that help you get involved. You can tell friends and family about YouTube videos they just can't miss and influence videos' ratings with your own view.

And if there's a chance your grandkids could get your iPad, you might appreciate the capability to flag inappropriate content on YouTube. (You need a YouTube account to use this feature.)

Sharing

1 Display a video in the YouTube app's reduced view, tap the video area to see the onscreen controls, and tap the Share button.

2 For e-mail, in the form that appears, enter a recipient in the To field and add to the message if you like. For Twitter, type in your accompanying message. Tap the Send button to send a link to the video. Then choose Mail Link to This Video to e-mail it or Tweet to tweet it.

TIP

If you like a video enough to share it, you might also be interested in the Comments feature. With a video displayed, tap the Comments tab. Tap in the Add a Comment field, type your comment, and tap the Send button on your keyboard. Your comment is posted.

Rating and flagging

1 Display a video in the YouTube app's reduced view, tap the video area to see the onscreen controls, and tap the Like or Dislike button, based on your evaluation of it.

2 If you're not already signed in to YouTube, you'll be asked to do so before your evaluation is counted.

TIP

To flag inappropriate content, begin with the video open in the YouTube app's reduced view. Tap in the video area near the top of the screen to display the onscreen controls. Next, tap the Flag button and then the Flag As Inappropriate menu option that appears. Enter the username and password for your account if you're not already signed in.

AirPlay and Video-Out

- *Devices you need **besides** your iPad* ● *Streaming media* ● *The scoop on cables*

The iPad makes for a pretty sweet video screen for watching movies, TV shows, and YouTube videos, and its speakers (or a pair of headphones) do a decent job playing music. But if you want to share your videos or music with others, you can — even on the big screen. The iPad provides various routes for playing video and audio through other devices: You can use the AirPlay feature to wirelessly stream video or audio, or you can use a special cable to play video on a TV or music through a stereo.

To use AirPlay, you need an AirPlay-compatible receiver, TV, projector, or other device for the iPad to stream the music or video to, and both your iPad and that device need to be on the same Wi-Fi network. The best known AirPlay receiver is Apple's own Apple TV (the $99 second- or third-generation, black model), which you can then connect to a TV, stereo, or home theater.

With a third-gen iPad or an iPad 2, you can also display your entire iPad screen on a device connected directly via a VGA or HDMI cable. This is great for showing people what's happening on your iPad.

Either way, if you have the original iPad, you can't mirror your display. Instead, only apps written to allow video output — YouTube, the Parallels remote control app, the Presenter browser, and so on — will transmit their screens to the external display device.

You aren't limited to using Apple TV as your AirPlay receiver. Other companies have AirPlay speakers and even AirPlay-enabled stereos available, so you don't need an intermediary like the Apple TV at all.

Streaming with AirPlay

After your AirPlay device is on and set up on your network, you should see a new option in the iPad's Videos, YouTube, and Music apps: an icon (usually near the Play button) that looks like a TV screen with a triangle at its base. Tap that icon, and a menu pops up to show you all available output devices, such as iPad and Apple TV. Tap the desired AirPlay device and your video or audio is sent to that device. It's that simple. (Of course, be sure your stereo or TV is set to the correct input to get the signal from the AirPlay device.)

The AirPlay icon appears when you're in range of an AirPlay output device. Tap it and select one.

Trying Out Home Sharing

The iPad lets you share your music libraries with other computers using iTunes, as well as with Apple TVs and other iPads on the same network — plus you can access their music. The

Turn your iPad into a remote control

If you want to use your iPad as a remote control for the Apple TV, follow these steps:

1. Download the free Remote app from the App Store.

2. In the app, turn on Home Sharing to get a list of available shared libraries and Apple TVs. Tap the Apple TV icon to control it and see your available libraries.

3. Tap a library from the list at left to access its videos and music files. Or, tap the Control button (the icon composed of four arrows) at the bottom right of the screen to use your iPad as a remote for the Apple TV.

key is to enter the same Home Sharing ID on all the devices you want to link this way. On the iPad, enter the ID in the Settings app: Tap Music from the list at left and enter the Home Sharing ID and password. **Note:** These may not be the same as your iTunes account username and password.

Connecting via Cables

You can send audio from your iPad to another device via a good old-fashioned audio cable, which you connect to the iPad's standard 1/8-inch audio jack at the bottom of the device. Your home stereo may use different connectors, such as RCA, in which case you'd get the appropriate cable for that. When you plug in the audio cable, the audio goes through it rather than through the iPad's built-in speaker.

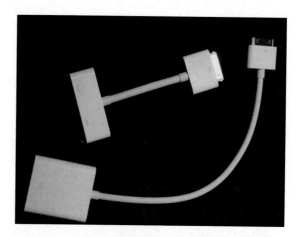

Apple's HDMI cable (left) and VGA cable (right)

For video, you have two cable options, both of which plug into the iPad's dock connector:

- ✔ **VGA:** Apple sells a $29 VGA cable to connect monitors, many TVs, and projectors to the iPad. When you do, the video is automatically sent through the cable instead of to the iPad's screen. Instead of the video, the iPad screen displays the basic playback controls. The screen also shows the AirPlay icon you use to switch the video back to the iPad. (Just tap the AirPlay button and choose the Dock Connector option.)

- ✔ **HDMI:** A $39 HDMI cable connects to newer TVs and newer projectors. When you connect an HDMI cable to the iPad, you use the AirPlay icon to switch the video to the HDMI cable — it's not automatic. Copy-protected videos, such as those you buy or rent via iTunes, will not display over the VGA cable. You need to use an HDMI cable for such videos (version 1.2 or later).

Making Your Own Movies

Let loose your inner Spielberg! Among the many things you can do on an iPad is edit movies. All you need is Apple's $4.99/£2.99 iMovie app and your creativity. iMovie is a very simple app to use, making movie-making accessible in a way you may have not thought possible for home movies, web videos, and even in-house training.

You can create two kinds of movies in iMovie:

- **Projects:** These are what most people think of as movies: edited videos with optional music and voice-overs.

- **Trailers:** Promo movies that use segments of a movie along with credits and text labels that introduce each clip.

To make either kind of movie, tap the Add (+) button in iMovie's documents view (the splash screen with the big marquee) and then choose either New Project or New Trailer, as desired.

From that splash screen, you can import video and

iMovie

(from a Mac) iMovie projects from iTunes by tapping the Import icon (the arrow-in-a-tray icon). Select an existing project or trailer by scrolling through their preview images so the marquee frame is around the one you want; then tap the desired one to open it, tap the Play icon to play it, or tap the Share icon to send the movie to the Photos app, iTunes, YouTube, Facebook, Vimeo, or CNN's iReport.

Working with Projects

When you open or create a movie project, a list of available video appears in the upper left. Tap a desired clip and then its Insert icon (a curved down arrow) to add it to the project. Notice the magenta line in the project window at the bottom of iMovie; that indicates your current location in the project timeline.

1. Add more clips as desired to the timeline. They'll appear before or after the clip where the current timeline location is, depending on which edge is closest to the timeline location.

2. To use just a portion of a video clip, tap the clip in the project timeline and then drag the yellow start and end lines inward, removing the portion of the clip outside the lines.

3. To move a clip, tap it and then drag it to the new location in the timeline. Be careful, though: If you drag it outside the timeline, it's removed from the timeline.

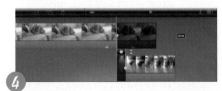

4. To insert a transition between clips, tap the horizontal double-arrow icon between them and then tap the vertical double-arrow icon that appears. Adjust the overlap by dragging the yellow handles on either or both clips as desired. Tap the vertical double-arrow icon to apply the overlap.

You should know these additional controls for editing a movie project:

- **Documents:** Tap the icon of a document in the top tool-bar to see your other projects and trailers. (iMovie saves your changes automatically.)

- **Undo:** Tap the curved-arrow icon at the right side of the top toolbar.

- **Settings:** Tap the gear icon at the right side of the top toolbar to add theme music, loop the background music, and control the fade-in and fade-out.

- **Media selectors:** The three icons at the left side of the toolbar above the project timeline let you choose videos from Photos, images from Photos, and music from Music.

- **Audio track:** Tap the pulse-like icon near the center of the project timeline's toolbar to show or hide the audio track below the project timeline.

- **Record:** Tap the microphone icon to record audio and the camera icon to record video (except for the original iPad) at the right side of the project timeline's toolbar.

Working with Trailers

iMovie offers several templates for creating movie trailers. They're highly formatted, and you can't remove or add elements to them; you can just change their text and choose the video clips to substitute for the placeholders.

To choose a template, tap the Add (+) icon in the documents splash screen, choose New Trailer, and tap the desired template from the scrolling preview icons at the bottom of the window that appears; then tap Create.

A trailer has two components, which you access via tabs:

- **Outline:** Tap the various fields here to edit the trailer title and all the various credits shown at the end.

- **Storyboard:** This is the predefined timeline for your trailer. Tap the text fields to edit their text and tap the video placeholders to select the video clips to use.

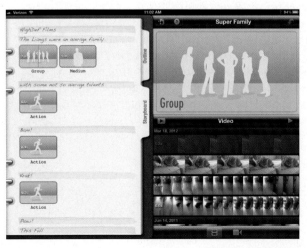

Editing an iMovie trailer

Discovering Apps

- *The breadth and depth of apps* • *Looking for apps* • *Buying apps*
- *Reporting on and reviewing apps*

One of the best things about the iPad is that you can download and install apps (short for *applications*) created by all sorts of developers, from programmers working in a garage to full-blown companies. More than 550,000 apps are available in the Apple iTunes App Store. Although most of those are for the iPhone and iPod touch, they all run on the iPad as well. Plus you can find more than 170,000 apps designed specifically for the iPad (many have "for iPad" or "HD" in the app name), plus tens of thousands more *hybrid* apps that adjust their user interface based on whether you're running them on an iPad or on an iPhone (or iPod touch). Hybrid apps are indicated by the + icon.

Both the iTunes App Store and the App Store app charge the purchases to your iTunes account. (If you don't have one, sign up via iTunes on your computer or iPad.) Prices range from free to nearly $200/£150, though most are just a few dollars or pounds. Some apps are useful, but others are lame; some apps are perfectly well-behaved, but others quit unexpectedly (or worse). Apps range from games to financial tools and productivity apps. The range of apps is amazing, but their quality range is wide, too.

TIP

When you access the iTunes Store via your computer, the App Store link near the top of the screen is also a pop-up menu (as are most of the other department links to its left and right). If you click and hold on most of these department links, a menu with a list of the department's categories appears. For example, if you click and hold on the App Store link, you can choose specific categories such as Books, Entertainment, and others from the pop-up menu, allowing you to bypass the App Store home page and go directly to that category. In the App Store app on the iPad, tap the Categories button to narrow your app search.

Getting Hold of Apps

You can obtain and install apps for your iPad from the App Store via iTunes on your computer or via the App Store app on your iPad (when it's connected to the Internet). Apps downloaded to the iPad are immediately available for use; apps downloaded to your computer don't get onto your iPad until you sync them from your computer or download them from your iPad (by going to the Purchased pane in the App Store app). When you sync your iPad and your computer, any apps purchased on one are synced to the other. If you also

*...keep your **apps updated** on all your **iOS devices**...*

own an iPhone or iPod touch, any apps you buy (other than iPad-only apps) are also synced to and from it.

So it's easy to keep your apps updated on all your iOS devices and backed up on your computer. Better yet, you don't have to keep the same apps on both your iPad and iPhone (and/or iPod touch). If you delete an app from your iPhone, for example, it remains on your iPad unless you delete it there as well. You can delete apps directly on an iOS device or in the Apps pane for that device in iTunes on your computer.

Locate apps with your computer

On your computer, use iTunes to find and buy iPad apps. The process is the same as for iTunes music and video. Follow these steps:

TIP

Apps you download are placed on additional Home screens, and you have to scroll to view and use them unless you move them to the dock, which makes them visible on all Home screens. Note that the dock can hold six apps maximum.

1 Launch iTunes and click the iTunes Store link in the Sidebar on the left.

2 Click the App Store button near the top of the page, and the iTunes App Store appears. To look only for apps designed to run at the full resolution of your iPad, click the iPad button at the top of the window.

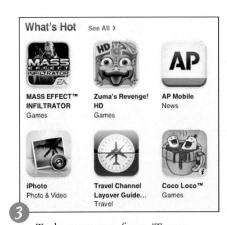

3 To buy an app from iTunes, just click its price button (which may say *Free*). The app begins downloading immediately if you're signed in to your iTunes account, and your credit card is charged; otherwise, you're first asked to provide your password and perhaps your username.

REMEMBER

After the app is downloaded to your computer, sync your iPad to transfer the app to it. It is placed on the first Home screen that has room for it — well, the first available Home screen after the first Home screen, which the iPad reserves for its default apps.

Explore the App Store

After you have the iTunes App Store on your screen, you have several options for exploring its virtual departments. The main departments are featured in the middle of the screen, and ancillary departments appear on either side of them:

✔ **New and Noteworthy** has 12 visible icons representing apps that are — what else? — new and noteworthy. Look to the right of the words *New and Noteworthy.* See the words *See All?* That's a link; if you click it, you see *all* apps in this department on a single screen. Or, you can click and drag the scroll bar to the right to see more icons.

✔ **What's Hot** displays 12 icons, though you can see only six of them representing apps that are popular with other iPad users. ***Note:*** You also see ads for four featured apps between the New and Noteworthy department and the What's Hot department.

✔ **Staff Favorites** appears below the What's Hot department, with Apple employees' suggestions.

Three other departments appear to the right, under the Top Charts heading: Paid Apps, one of my favorite departments; Free Apps; and Top Grossing Apps. The Number 1 app in each department displays both its icon and its name; the next nine apps show text links only.

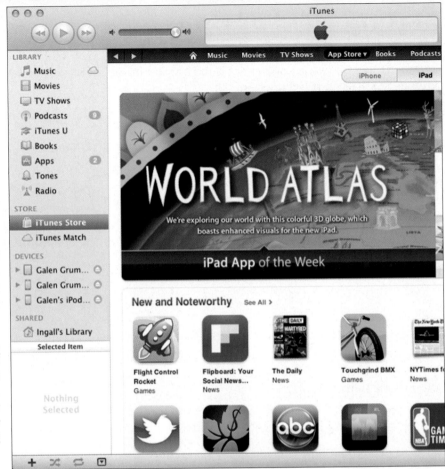

TIP

The little triangle to the right of each item's price opens a pop-up menu if clicked. Its options let you give this app to someone as a gift, add it to your wish list, send an e-mail to a friend with a link to it, copy the link to this product to the Clipboard so that you can paste it elsewhere, or share this item on Facebook or Twitter.

Browsing the screen is helpful, but if you know exactly what you're looking for, it's easier to just search for it by typing all or part of its name in the Search field in the upper-right corner of the main iTunes window. Then press Enter or Return to initiate the search. The bad news is that the search goes across the entire iTunes Store, which includes music, TV shows, movies, and other stuff in addition to iPad apps. Fortunately, search results are shown in categories — one of which is iPad Apps. Plus, if you click the See All link to the right of the words *iPad Apps,* all the iPad apps that match your search word or phrase appear on a single screen.

DUMMIES

Locate apps with your iPad

Finding apps with your iPad is almost as easy as finding them by using iTunes on your computer. The only requirement is that you have an Internet connection of some sort — Wi-Fi or cellular — so that you can access the iTunes App Store and browse, search, download, and install apps.

To get started, open the App Store app. After you launch the App Store, you see six buttons at the bottom of the screen, representing six ways to interact with the store. Three icons at the bottom of the screen — Featured, Top Charts, and Categories — offer three ways to browse the virtual departments of the App Store. The Genius icon creates a set of recommendations based on the apps you already own on your iPad; you have to have set up Genius on your computer's iTunes for this to work. (The fifth button, Purchases, shows you all apps you've bought and lets you download any not on the iPad. The sixth button, Updates, shows available updates to the apps you already have.)

Here's what each of these app-store departments offers:

- **Featured** has two panes, accessed via the tabs at the top of the screen: New and What's Hot.

- **Top Charts** offers lists of the Top Paid iPad apps and the Top Free iPad apps. In the upper-left corner of the Top Charts screen is a Categories button. You can tap it to see a list of categories such as Books, Education, Games, Music, News, and Productivity. Tap any of these categories to see its top paid and top free iPad apps.

- **Categories** works a little differently: It has no panes, and its main page contains no apps. Instead, it offers a list of categories such as Games, Entertainment, Utilities, Music, and Lifestyle, to name a few. Tap a category to see a page full of apps of that type.

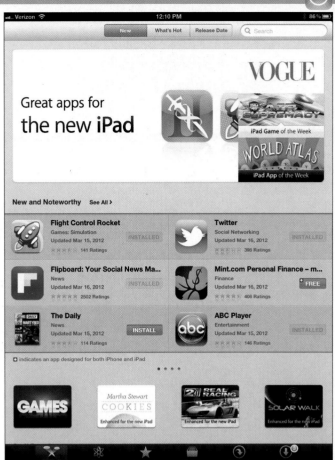

The App Store highlights new and recommended apps.

Most pages in the App Store display more apps than can fit on the screen at once. For example, the New and Noteworthy section contains more than six apps. A few tools help you navigate the multiple pages of apps:

- The little triangles at the top and bottom of the New and Noteworthy section are buttons you click to see the next or previous page of apps in that section. Tap them to see the next or previous page of apps.

- The little dots in the middle of the gray area above and below most sections tell you how many pages the section contains; the white dot indicates which page you're currently viewing.

- Tap the See All link at the top of most sections to (what else?) see all the apps in the section on the same screen.

You can also search for an app if you know all or part of the name. In the App Store app, tap in the Search field, enter a search term, and tap the Search button on the onscreen keyboard to see results.

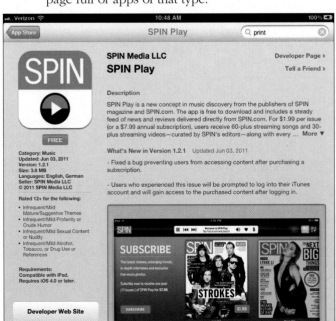

An app's detail page

To buy an app from your iPad, follow these steps:

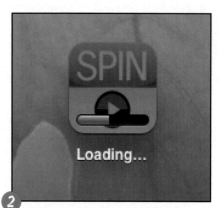

1 Tap the price button (which may say Free) near the top of its detail screen. The price button is then replaced by a green rectangle that says *Install App*. Tap the Install App button.

2 When prompted, type your iTunes Store account password. The App Store closes, and you see the Home screen where the new app's icon will reside. As it's downloading, the new app's icon is slightly dimmed and has the word *Loading* beneath it and a blue progress bar near its bottom.

Using iPhone apps on your iPad

The trend is for app developers to create hybrid apps that look one way on the iPhone and iPod touch's smaller screen (320 x 480 pixels) and another way on the iPad's large screen (2,048 x 1,536 pixels for the third-gen iPad and 1,024 x 768 pixels for the previous models). In the App Store, these hybrid apps have a plus (+) symbol next to their price.

When you run a nonhybrid iPhone app on the iPad, it's displayed in a 320-x-480-pixel window, as if there were an iPhone embedded in your screen, as shown in the left image. You can double the size of such an iPhone app (as shown in the image on the right) by tapping the 2X button in the lower-right corner of the screen; to return it to its native size, tap the 1X button that takes its place.

Most iPhone apps look pretty good at the 2X size, but a few have jagged graphics and don't look as nice. Also, when you run an iPhone app on your iPad, your iPad screen needs to be in portrait orientation — the iPhone app won't rotate horizontally with your iPad.

REMEMBER

If the app is rated 17+, click OK in the warning screen that appears after you type your password to confirm that you're older than 17 before the app downloads. **Note:** Apple regards any app that accesses Internet or entertainment content as "adult" because users can find mature content through them. Thus, apps you may consider to be innocuous, such as alternative browsers, are flagged as 17+.

DUMMIES

Working with previous purchases

In the Purchases pane of the App Store, you get a list of all apps you've bought for any iOS device you own. Tap iPad to see just iPad apps and iPhone to see just iPhone apps. (Hybrid apps appear in both lists.) Any apps not installed on your iPad display a cloud icon button to the right of their description; tap that button to download the app to your iPad. (You won't be charged to re-download an app.)

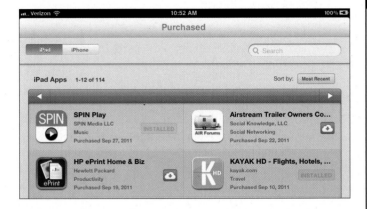

Reading app reviews

Whether you're looking at an app on your computer via the iTunes App Store or in the iPad's App Store app, if you scroll down the detail screen of an app, near the bottom you find a series of customer reviews written by users of this app. Each review includes a star rating, from zero to five. If an app is rated four or higher by a reasonable number of people, that means the app is well-liked by people who actually use it.

You see a few more reviews with star ratings below the review. If you care to read even more reviews than are shown on the detail page, on iTunes, click the small buttons on the right side of the Customer Reviews section — Back, one or more page numbers, and Next — to navigate to the pages of comments for this app. On the iPad, tap More.

Finally, just above these icons is a pop-up Sort By menu that says Most Helpful. This menu lets you sort the customer reviews by your choice of Most Helpful, Most Favorable, Most Critical, or Most Recent.

Reviewing an app

Sometimes you love or hate an application so much that you want to tell the world about it. In that case, you should write a review. You can do this from two locations: in iTunes on your computer or directly from your iPad.

To write a review using iTunes, follow these steps:

1. Navigate to the detail page for the application in the iTunes App Store.

2. Scroll down the page to the Reviews section and click the Write a Review link. You probably have to type your iTunes Store password at this point.

3. Click the button for the star rating you want to give the application.

4. In the Title field, type a title for your review.

5. In the Review field, type your review.

6. Click the Submit button when you're finished. The Preview screen appears. If the review looks good to you, you're done. If you want to change something, click the Edit button.

To write a review from your iPad, follow these steps:

1. Tap the App Store icon to launch the App Store.

2. Navigate to the detail screen for the application.

3. Scroll down the page and tap the Write a Review link. You probably have to type your iTunes Store password at this point.

4. Tap one to five of the stars at the top of the Write a Review screen to rate the application.

5. In the Title field, type a title for your review.

6. In the Review field, type your review.

7. Tap the Submit button in the upper-right corner of the screen.

Whichever way you submit your review, Apple reviews your submission. As long as it doesn't violate the (unpublished) rules of conduct for app reviews, it appears in a day or two in the App Store, in the Reviews section for the particular application.

The Free Apps That Should Be Standard

Although the iPad comes with a lot of apps, there are several other free apps that you'll rely on and that should be your first downloads from the App Store after you buy an iPad:

- **iBooks:** The iPad makes a great e-reader, and Apple sells lots of e-books at its iBookstore. But to read them, you need Apple's free iBooks app. You'll likely also want Amazon.com's Kindle app to read books from that e-book-store as well.

- **Twitter:** iOS 5 integrates Twitter into its Share menus for Mail, Photos, Safari, and YouTube apps. But it doesn't come with the Twitter app for you to monitor your tweets, retweet messages, direct-message others, and so on.

- **Find My iPhone:** Another feature built into the iPad's iOS is the ability to report its location, so if your iPad is lost or stolen, you can locate its current (or at least last-known) location, send a message to the device, and even lock or wipe it. But you can also use the iPad to track and similarly manage your Macs and other iOS devices — if you download this app, that is.

- **iTunes U:** Formerly part of the Music and Videos apps, this library of free audio and video lectures from renowned educators throughout the world is now its own app.

iPhone owners may notice that the iPad lacks several apps that come with the iPhone, including a stock tracker, weather tracker, clock, and calculator. Later in this book, I list all sorts of handy apps such as these — some free, some not — that you should consider adding to your iPad.

GarageBand

Apple's Apps for the Apple Universe

Apple makes several other apps that you should consider bringing to your iPad, especially if you use Macs in addition to your iPad, iPhone, and/or iPod touch.

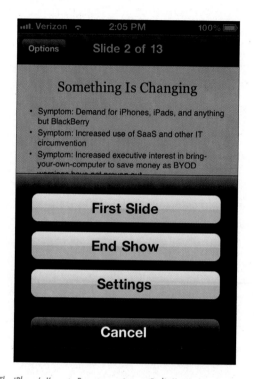

The iPhone's Keynote Remote running an iPad's Keynote presentation

AirPort Utility

✔ **Remote:** This free app lets you control your Apple TV from any iOS device, turning it into a remote control for iTunes content obtained through the Apple TV or sent to your TV from your computer's iTunes via the Apple TV.

✔ **iWork suite:** The trio of Pages, Keynote, and Numbers ($9.99/£6.99 each) lets you work not only with Apple's iWork files created on your Mac but also with Microsoft Office files anywhere. You can also create both iWork and Office documents on your iPad with iWork, and iWork uses iCloud to keep your documents synced with your Mac and other iOS devices automatically. The free Keynote Remote app for iPhone lets your iPhone or iPod touch act as a remote control for your Keynote presentation whether on a Mac or an iPad, if they're all on the same Wi-Fi network.

✔ **iLife suite:** One of the big advantages of the Mac is the iLife suite that's included for free on new systems: iMovie for movie editing, GarageBand for music creation, and iPhoto for image retouching. All three now have iOS versions ($4.99/£2.99 each), so you can create and edit media files on your iPad, as well as move them among your Mac and iOS devices via iTunes; photos also can be synced via iCloud. (iPhoto doesn't work on an original iPad.) It's amazing what these apps can do on an iPad.

✔ **AirPort Utility:** If you use any of Apple's Wi-Fi routers (the AirPort Extreme, AirPort Express, or Time Capsule) in your network, you can manage them from your iPad with this free utility. Too bad you can't manage other manufacturers' Wi-Fi routers as well!

Managing Apps

When you have a bunch of apps on your iPad (people usually start asking that question after they've filled up their first Home screen), you'll start to wonder how to manage them. The iPad provides many ways to manage your apps, including ways to rearrange their location, to delete ones not used, and more. You can also manage apps on your computer via iTunes, which is particularly handy if you're also managing apps on other devices such as an iPhone linked to the same iTunes account.

TIP

If you try to update an application purchased from any iTunes Store account except your own, you're prompted for that account's ID and password. If you can't provide them, you can't download the update.

Getting Updates

Every so often, the developer of an iPad app releases an update. Sometimes these updates add new features to the app, sometimes they squash bugs, and sometimes they do both. In any event, updates are usually a good thing for you and your iPad, so it makes sense to check for them every so often.

On the iPad, if there are updates available, a red circle with a number in it (called a badge) appears next to the App Store icon; that number indicates how many updates are available. Tap the Updates button to open the list of available updates. Then tap Update next to each app you want to update or tap Update All to update them all.

Another way of knowing that you have updates waiting is to look at the little number in a circle next to the Apps item in the iTunes Sidebar. Click that item to open a window showing the available updates. To update iPad apps from iTunes on your computer, click the Check for Updates link near the lower-right corner of the Apps pane. Note that if any updates are available, this link tells you how many.

To grab any update, click the Download All Free Updates button or click the Get Update button next to each app. After you download an update this way, it replaces the version on your iPad automatically the next time you sync.

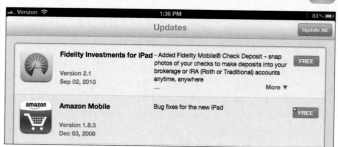

Delete from iTunes

To delete an app from iTunes, click Apps in the Sidebar and then do one of the following:

- Click the app in the main window to select it and press the Backspace or Delete key.
- Click the app to select it and then choose Edit⇨Delete.
- Right-click (or Control-click on a Mac) the app and choose Delete.

You see a dialog box that asks whether you're sure. If you click the Remove button, the app is removed from your iTunes library, as well as from any iPad that syncs with it.

Delete Apps from the iPad

Deleting an app from your iPad doesn't get rid of it permanently: It remains in your iTunes library until you delete it from iTunes. Put another way: Even though you deleted the app from your iPad, it's still in your iTunes library. If you want to get rid of an app for good, you must also delete it from your iTunes library. To delete an app directly on your iPad, take these steps:

1 Press and hold any icon until all the icons begin to wiggle.

2 Tap the X-in-a-circle icon in the upper-left corner of the app that you want to delete. A dialog box tells you that deleting this app also deletes all its data.

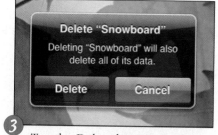

3 Tap the Delete button. To stop the icons from wiggling, just press the Home or Sleep/Wake button.

Rearranging Apps on Your Computer

In iTunes on your computer, you can rearrange iPad apps. Click your iPad in the Sidebar's Devices list and then go to the Apps pane. You see a list of apps at the left of the main screen and an image of your Home screens on the right of the main screen. You can deselect an app from the list to remove it from the iPad (but not the iTunes library), and you can drag app icons within the Home screens to move their location. The changes are made on your iPad the next time you sync.

Rearranging Apps on Your iPad

1 To move an app's icon on the iPad, tap and press any app until all the apps begin to wiggle.

3 Press the Home button to stop the wiggling.

2 Now drag any app icon to a new location on the current or another Home screen.

- Drag the icon between two apps to insert it between them.

- Drag the icon off the left or right edge of the screen to move to the previous or next Home screen.

- Drag app icons to and from the Dock at the bottom of the screen so they appear on every Home screen. The Dock can hold up to six apps.

Managing app storage

iOS 5 lets you see and manage the storage used by each app. In the Settings app, go to the General pane and tap Usage. A list of all apps and their storage use displays. Tap an app to get more details and, for compatible apps, delete individual files to make more room available.

DUMMIES

Using App Folders

iOS lets you create app folders to contain multiple apps, which can reduce the number of Home screens to scroll through — folders also let you add apps when you fill up the 11 Home screens. The process is easy: Tap and hold an app until the apps start to wiggle. Then just drag one app onto another. The iPad creates a folder that contains both apps. By default, the folder gets the name of the first app's category, but you can edit the name in the text field that appears.

To access an app in a folder, simply tap it. A window opens at the bottom showing all the apps; just tap the one you want to launch it.

Tap a folder to open a window showing each app in it; tap outside the folder to close it.

To remove an app from a folder, tap and hold it in the open folder window until the apps begin to wiggle. Then drag the app out of the window and into the Home screen.

Switching Apps

When you tap an app's icon to run it, the rest of the iPad screen disappears. There's no menu or Dock as in Mac OS X to help you switch to other apps, nor is there a Start menu or taskbar as in Windows. So how do you return to your Home screen and switch to another app? You have two options:

✔ Press the Home button or (in iOS 5) pinch with your thumb and three fingers to get back to the Home screen; then tap another app to open it. Note that the app you left behind either keeps running in the background or suspends itself. Most suspended apps save any data that was open.

✔ Double-press the Home button or (in iOS 5) swipe up with four fingers to open or close the multitasking dock that shows other running apps. Tap one of those to open it; your current app remains running and will display in the window. (Apps continue to run until you press and hold an app within the apps bar and then tap the minus-in-a-circle icon to close it.)

✔ In iOS 5, swipe to the right or left with four fingers to move from one running app to the next. The sequence matches that of the multitasking dock's app list.

If the new app-switching gestures in iOS 5 don't work, go to the Settings app's General pane and be sure the Multitasking Gestures switch is set to On.

The apps bar of running apps appears when you double-press the Home button

A Gallery of Apps

Safari Alternatives

Atomic Browser ($0.99/£0.69) provides full-screen web browsing, web agent switching (telling a site you're a desktop PC, so you're not stuck with mobile-optimized sites), tabbed panes, and more. **Mercury Web Browser Pro** ($0.99/£0.69) offers Firefox, customizable gestures, desktop browsing, ad blocking, and more desktop-like features. Even more desktop-like, consider **Perfect Browser** ($3.99/£2.49) for full-screen browsing, tabbed panes, offline viewing, desktop rendering, private browsing, VGA output (original iPad), and more.

If you're browsing at night with the lights off or dim, try **Night Browser**, which adjusts the screen display automatically to account for ambient light. (Free)

Mail Helpers

If your company uses Lotus Notes, check out IBM's **Lotus Notes Traveler** (free) app, which can connect to the very latest version of the Lotus Notes server. And if your company uses Novell's GroupWise, use the **GW Mail** ($9.99/£6.99) app to connect to GroupWise Server versions 6 through 8 for e-mail access — if WebAccess is enabled on GroupWise.

The iPad doesn't support the Zip format, which compresses files and lets you package several files into one container. But you're likely to get Zip format files in your e-mails. With **ZipThat** ($0.99/£0.69) installed, any zipped files you tap in e-mail open in a ZipThat window. Tap the Zip file's name to see its contents and tap any file within it to open it. Tap and hold to access the iPad's Open In feature. **Unzip** ($0.99/£0.69) is another option for opening Zip files. It works like ZipThat does. The **ZipBox-Pro** ($1.99/£1.49) app also unzips files but takes more steps than ZipThat and Unzip.

If you want to create form letters, consider **Mailer**. It lets you create e-mail templates that you can then fill in. You can also attach various kinds of files directly to your messages. ($3.99/£2.49)

Audio

Pandora Radio (free) is deservedly one of the most famous music apps, providing streaming access to millions of songs. Likewise, **Kazaa** (free) and **Spotify** (free) are essentially radio stations you can program to your preferences. Less known but with a strong following is **Wunder Radio** ($3.99/£2.49), a music-streaming app that provides accesses to hundreds of online radio stations.

GarageBand ($4.99/£2.99) is Apple's amazing sound-mixing and music-synthesizing app. **RJ Voyager** (free) lets you create song mixes with all sorts of cut and mix controls. You can also add visual scenes purchased from its online store. Relive the boom-box and mix-tape generation with **Jamboxx** (free), which lets you create playlists in iTunes with extra effects, such as volume changes, and then play them as your iPad screen simulates a boom box, complete with LED EQs.

More professionally inclined iPad users may want to investigate **StudioTrack**, a mixing app designed to produce high-quality recordings. ($9.99/£6.99)

Musicnotes Sheet Music Viewer (free) lets you read sheet music on your iPad while playing — if you have a Musicnotes.com account and Internet connection. **ForScore** ($4.99/£2.99) is a great music sheet reader that doesn't require your being online to use it.

Enhancers

If you're a drummer or dream of being one, check out **Shiny Drum** (free) and turn your iPad into a percussion player for all sorts of drum sounds. Learn to play, or practice playing, the piano with **Virtuoso Piano 2 HD** (free). Beginners and professional musicians alike may want to add **Nota** ($2.99/£1.99) to their toolkits for its piano chord and (even exotic) scale browser, piano and staff note locator, and note reference library.

British guitarist Ace has laid down a selection of loops that power **GrooveMaster Rock Ace**, an app that lets you build on these musical snippets to create your own songs. ($9.99/£6.99)

If you like the TV series Glee, you'll love **Glee Karaoke**, which lets you sing along (digitally enhanced as you do) with popular series tunes. (Free)

You're hearing a song and just can't remember what it is. **SoundHound** ($6.99/£4.99) can listen via your iPad and find out for you — and even connect you to the iTunes Store so you can buy it or similar songs. **Shazam** (free) can identify music for you, but it also lets you tag music and then follow other people's tags to help you find music you may like but not be aware of.

Video Aids

GoodPlayer ($2.99/£1.99) lets you watch video formats on your iPad that the iPad doesn't support natively. To stream videos from your computer to your iPad, use **Air Video** ($2.99/£1.99).

Use **Netflix** to watch movies and TV shows in your Netflix account's Instant Queue. Note the app does not let you manage your Netflix queues. (Free)

Watch an ever-changing selection of TV shows and other videos from the ABC-TV network using the **ABC Player** (free). If public television is more your style, watch its programming on the **PBS** (free) app.

The Hulu.com Web site provides TV shows from several networks, but it's not iPad-compatible. Fortunately, the **Hulu Plus** (free) app is. Don't know what's on TV tonight? Use the **TV Guide** (free) app to find out. Can't remember what movie that actress was so great in, use the **IMDb** app (free), a searchable guide to movies, television, actors, and more.

A handy way to control your TiVo or other compatible DVR uses **DVR Remote** ($2.99/£1.99). If you're a satellite TV subscriber, use the **Dish Remote** (free) app to control your Dish set-top box. Likewise, Comcast has the **Xfinity** (free) app for its cable subscribers to watch TV on the go.

To-Do's and Databases

The iPad's Reminders app provides basic to-do management capabilities, but if you want something more sophisticated, there are dozens of to-do list managers available for the iPad. Three to consider are **Todo for iPad** ($4.99/£2.99), **Task Pro** ($1.99/£1.49), and the **Toodledo** ($2.99/£1.99).

Project management requires a much more sophisticated approach to task and schedule management. One app to consider on the iPad for such work is **OmniFocus**. It syncs with the desktop version of the software, updates the Calendar app with due dates, and can show nearby task locations on a map. ($39.99/£27.99)

For a personal management tool, take a look at the **Bento for iPad** app, which is a lightweight database perfect for tracking records, contacts, to-do's, and other personal tasks and data. ($9.99/£6.99)

For work-oriented databases, an app worth considering is **HanDBase for iPad**. ($9.99/£6.99)

Note-Takers

If you prefer to write and draw notes with a stylus, check out **PaperDesk for iPad** ($3.99/£2.79) and **Penultimate** ($2.99/£0.69). Both apps let you send your visual notes as PDF files. (Looking for a stylus? TenOneDesign's Pogo Stylus is a great option.)

For heavy-duty note-taking, consider **Notes Plus** ($7.99/£5.49), which lets you mix typed text, stylus-written text and images, and voice recordings in your notes. It also smoothes out text as you write and zooms in for a closer view of cryptic results. **Note Taker HD** ($4.99/£2.99), a similar heavy-duty app, offers multisheet notes you can display on a monitor via a VGA connector.

The **Notability** app lets you record lectures and meetings. If you jot down notes during the recording, tap the text to play back what was being said at the time. ($4.99/£2.99)

If you need course-style note-taking, consider **Notebook for iPad**. This app lets you create extensive notes combining text, your own drawings, images from the Photos app, and audio recordings. ($1.99/£1.49)

Most style-based note-taking apps limit you to an image of your notes, rather than text you can copy and paste or search. **WritePad for iPad** is different: Its handwriting recognition converts what you write via a stylus into text. ($9.99/£6.99)

Outliners and Diagrammers

If you do mind-mapping — a method of organizing thoughts and items by their relationships — **iThoughts HD** could be the tool for you. It works with several mindmap formats and can export your mind maps to PNG and PDF formats. It also syncs to the Box.net and Dropbox cloud storage services. ($9.99/£6.99)

MindNode is another mind-mapping tool to consider. Among its capabilities is support for VGA output to a monitor if you have a VGA adapter for your iPad. ($9.99/£6.99)

If you're looking for a tool to do either mind-mapping or traditional whiteboarding, **Instaviz** is a strong option. ($9.99/£6.99)

For more traditional whiteboard sketching, give **Whiteboard HD** ($4.99/£2.99) a look. It gives you controls over labeling, provides a grid background, and supports image inclusion from the Photos app. **OmniGraph Sketcher** ($14.99/£10.49) is a good app for traditional diagramming and creating precision graphs for architecture, finance, engineering, and space planning.

For sophisticated diagramming of process charts, website wireframes, or other complex relationships, **OmniGraffle** is highly regarded. It supports freehand drawing but also has a bevy of intelligent controls to make items format quickly and snap to standard sizes and locations. Its files are compatible with the desktop version, and you can export PDF view-only versions as well. ($49.99/£34.99)

File

Box is a cloud storage service that offers free access to some file storage and charges for additional storage. Its iPad app lets several applications get files from and put files on its online storage server for access by your other devices and computers. (Free)

Dropbox is a cloud storage service very much like Box, with a free basic service and a paid extra-capacity service. (Free)

If you don't want to sync files over the Internet, consider **GoodReader for iPad** instead. It lets you send files from your Mac or PC to your iPad directly over Wi-Fi, as well as via iTunes. Plus it has PDF annotation capabilities and other handy on-the-go document-handling features. ($4.99/£2.99)

The Google Drive (formerly Google Docs) online software toolkit lets you work on text and spreadsheet documents on the Internet from your browser. Unfortunately, it is very difficult to use on an iPad. Although several apps let you open documents stored in Google Drive and send documents to it, the **GoDocs** app goes a step further and lets you actually edit those documents directly from your iPad. ($4.99/£2.99)

Sharers

A really cool device is the PogoPlug, which lets you attach a disk drive to your home network, making that drive accessible to you via the Internet. Think of it as your own cloud storage service, with no storage fees. (The device costs from $50/£40 to $100/£80, depending on the model.) The **PogoPlug HD** app lets your iPad access that drive's contents. (Free)

If you work with your own or clients' websites and need to send files to and from, **FTP On the Go Pro** will do the trick. It also lets you edit web pages and related files, so you can update your site from your iPad when you're on the go. ($9.99/£6.99)

Air Sharing lets you mount your iPad as if it were a drive on your computer, so you can transfer files to it. It also can read many files on your iPad, create and open Zip files, and connect to other users' whose devices have Air Sharing installed and are on the same wireless network. ($9.99/£6.99)

FileApp Pro is a file organizer for your iPad, letting you copy files to and from your iPad and then letting you organize, rename, move, and multiple-select files, as well as open them in compatible iPad applications. ($4.99/£2.99)

With **Server Admin Remote** ($9.99/£6.99), IT staff can monitor Mac OS X Servers from their iPads. And **LogMeIn Ignition** ($99.99/£69.99) is a remote-access/screen-sharing app that lets you remote-control your Windows PC or Mac over the Internet.

Enterprise Clients

Citrix Receiver for iPad lets you run Office, SharePoint, and other data center apps on your iPad through a virtual window to your Citrix-enabled servers. (Free)

If you want to run applications on your Mac or Windows PC, or on remote servers, from your iPad, consider **Wyse PocketCloud** ($11.99/£7.99). It allows remote control of a PC from your iPad. Another way to remote-control a PC or Mac to run its applications from an iPad is with the **Mocha VNC** ($5.99/£3.99) app. **Connect My PC** ($4.99/£2.99) is aimed at people who need to run just Windows desktops remotely from their iPad. Multiple connections are allowed.

FileMaker Go for iPad lets your iPad access and control FileMaker databases running on a FileMaker server. ($19.99/£13.99 Version for 11, free for Version 12)

Many businesses use Microsoft SharePoint to enable collaboration over Office files. **SharePlus Office Mobile Client** ($19.99/£13.99) lets iPads be part of that collaboration. If you don't need the ability to edit documents via SharePoint, consider getting **Moprise** (free). It lets you view SharePoint-provisioned documents, and cut and paste their text into your other iPad applications.

Mobile CRM+ gives iPad users direct access to a Microsoft Dynamics CRM server, so they can manage and monitor customer relationship and sales transactions on the go. ($99.99 U.S. only)

Mobile Edge for Microsoft Dynamics, **NetSuite**, **Siebel CRM**, and **SugarCRM** are all client apps that let you connect into popular CRM and ERP systems. (Prices vary based on number of licenses.)

SAP BusinessObjects Explorer (free) lets you connect into SAP's business intelligence tool to explore sales trends and share the results with colleagues. Similarly, **Oracle Business Intelligence Mobile** (free) provides access to Oracle's BI server.

With **MicroStrategy Mobile for iPad**, you can access performance and other metric dashboards set up in a MicroStrategy business intelligence server. (Free)

Analyze your Excel, Google Drive, or Salesforce.com data visually with **Roambi Visualizer**. (Licenses start at $99/£79 per user per year.) If you run a website whose traffic you monitor with Google Analytics, **Analytics HD** ($6.99/£4.99) lets you track that traffic and run reports from your iPad.

Access your SQL database, run queries, and manage records from your iPad using **SQLTouch**. ($1.99/£1.49)

Business travelers who use the Concur travel service can track their trips and always have the details available through the **Concur Mobile** app. (Free)

Everyday Apps

Cooking, Dining, Etc.

Are you having trouble figuring out tips or splitting restaurant bills? **CheckPlease** (free) makes it easy. It even stores your local sales tax so it can just calculate the tip based on the total bill.

When you're looking for a restaurant and want to make a reservation to boot, **OpenTable** (free) makes recommendations and reservations over your Internet connection. **Urbanspoon** (free) is a restaurant finder with a built-in slot machine-like tool; shake the iPad (or tap a button), and it randomly picks any or all of three criteria — neighborhood, cuisine, and price — to make a recommendation.

Love to eat but need help when it comes to preparing a great meal? **Epicurious** can help you find a yummy recipe in no time. When you do, add it to a collection of Favorites, e-mail it to a friend, pass ingredients to your shopping list, or summon nutritional info. (Free)

Photo Cookbook: Quick and Easy uses extensive photography to show you how to cook rather than just follow recipe instructions. Learn to cook meals that take less than 30 minutes each. ($4.99 /£2.99)

Manage your exercise and diet regime more easily with **Calorie Tracker**. ($2.99/£1.99)

Education

Earth Flags HD helps you find out about world geography and national flags. ($1.99/£1.49)

Use **Google Earth** to explore the world via satellite maps that you can zoom in and out of easily — and even search for locations by name or address — as long as you have an Internet connection. (Free)

Kindergarten and elementary school students can sharpen their math skills with the **MathBoard** learning app. ($4.99/£2.99)

Monkey Preschool Lunchbox is an educational game for preschool students that teaches them about colors, shapes, and counting. ($0.99/£0.69)

Learn the skies easily with **Pocket Universe HD** ($2.99/£1.99). By using the iPad's location detection and compass features, this app can "see" the sky you're looking at and show you the constellations and more. Explore the solar system in 3D with **Solar Walk** ($2.99/£1.99).

Apple's iTunes U (free) provides access to thousands of audio and video lectures from educators worldwide, all at no charge.

Entertainment

Comics is actually three apps rolled into one: It's a fantastic way to read comic books on a 9.7-inch touchscreen; it's a comic book store with hundreds of comics and series from dozens of publishers; and it's a great way to organize the comics you own to find the one you want quickly and easily. (Free; comics issues typically cost $0.99–$4.99)

Drawing Pad, aimed at kids, this app lets them draw with virtual crayons to create original images or embellish imported photos. ($1.99/£1.49)

Get creative with **Paint Studio**! Use this powerful app to draw, add color, and even create special effects. If you don't need all those features, try Paint Studio Jr. ($1.99/£1.49)

Finance

Do all sorts of business calculations with **Financial Calculator**. Figure cash flow, annuity growth, amortization, you name it. ($2.99/£1.99)

Manage all your bills and accounts through the **Money for iPad** central financial management console. ($9.99/£6.99)

Keep track of your investments on your iPad with **Stocks Portfolio for iPad**. You can use it to create a watch list and record your stocks' performance. ($9.99/£6.99)

Fun and Games

Most people have played air hockey in a college rec hall, tavern, or roller rink. The iPad's large display, smooth graphics, and realistic sounds make **Air Hockey Gold** the next-best thing. Enjoy one- or two-player versions or play wirelessly via Bluetooth against a pal who also has the app. (Free)

Casino for iPad is a gambling emporium you can take with you. It has roulette, blackjack, poker, and seven other games. ($4.99/£2.99)

The classic drawing game comes to the iPad with **Etch a Sketch HD**. You can even save and share your drawings. ($2.99/£1.99)

Flight Control HD, one of the most popular iPhone games, is also on the iPad. It has high-res graphics and new flight courses. ($4.99/£2.99)

Manage and play as any of the 32 teams, with 2,000 players from the 2011-12 season, in **NFL 2012 HD's** realistic simulation game (free, but plenty of extras to buy). If you're a fan of the original football (soccer), **The Football App HD** (free) is chock-full of stats, tickers, and more.

Fans of MMORPG-style gaming can get **Pocket Legends for iPad**, an incredibly cool 3D game that doesn't have to cost a cent. Join players worldwide and wander dungeons, forests, and castles while collecting gold pieces and killing zombies and other bad guys. (Free, but with plenty of extras to buy)

Chances are good that you play Solitaire on your computer. Get **Real Solitaire** ($1.99/£1.49) for your iPad and do the same there! If you prefer mental math puzzles, try out **Sudoku HD** ($2.99/£1.99) on your iPad. Levels range from easy to hard for variety, and playing makes time fly by in the dentist's waiting room.

Scrabble for iPad ($9.99/£6.99) takes this classic game wherever you do, with no worries about losing the letter pieces. **T Chess Pro** ($7.99/£5.49) lets you play against a real person or a computerized master-class opponent for fun or to sharpen your skills.

Starfall HD ($4.99/£2.99), a tower defense game in a futuristic setting, tests your strategic abilities in an action-packed universe. Create and run your own universe in **Osmos** ($4.99/£2.99), a game that is part physics experiment and part Darwinist game of survival.

Photography

PhotoCalc helps photographers calculate exposure reciprocation, depth of field, and flash exposure. ($2.99/£1.99)

To make your photos more interesting, check out **CameraBag**, which lets you enhance your photos using many classic camera and film simulations. ($1.99/£1.49)

Use **LensFlare HD** to add optical effects to your photos, include SLR lens flares, subtle glints, sunlight flares, and the cinematic anamorphic lens flares made famous in the 2009 *Star Trek* film. ($2.99/£1.99)

It's a one-trick pony, but the trick is fun: **Photo Splash Effects** lets you convert a photo to grayscale and colorize one element to dramatically stand out. ($0.99/£0.69)

Adobe's Photoshop Touch ($9.99/£6.99) brings to the iPad the core features of the standard desktop image editor, including layer support, filters, and image adjustments. (It is not available for the original iPad.) **PhotoForge 2** ($3.99/£1.99) is a powerful image-editing app edits photos, applies filters and effects, and offers tools to create illustrations and paintings from scratch.

Apple's iPhoto ($4.99/£2.99) provides sophisticated but easy-to-use retouching and effects for your photos. (It is not available for original iPad.) **Snapseed** ($4.99/£2.99) also provides a capable set of retouching features, as well as some fun filters. **Photogene** ($2.99/£1.99) helps you improve your digital photos via a set of editing tools that crop, straighten, sharpen, adjust color, and correct underexposed photos. It also lets you upload photos to Flickr and FTP servers.

The original iPad has no camera, but that's not an issue if you have an iPhone and the **Camera** app for iPad. This app gives the iPad wireless access to the iPhone's camera; your iPad displays what the iPhone camera is seeing. ($0.99/£0.69)

Science and Medicine

Elektor Electronic Toolbox gives you more than a dozen calculators plus handy reference material for electrical projects. ($5.99/£2.99)

Use **Symbolic Calculator HD**, a powerful scientific calculator, to create and solve algebraic equations. ($1.99/£1.49)

Use the **Mediquations Medical Calculator** to help you calculate medications using built-in formulas and read scores for various medications. Check with your physician before using! ($4.99/£2.99)

Get access to information on thousands of drugs with this pharmacist-curated online reference guide, **PocketPharmacist** ($2.99/£1.49).

Wolfram Alpha ($2.99/£1.99; add-in modules available) is a knowledge navigator that answers your questions and performs computations in a variety of disciplines based on your queries.

Utilities

Turn your iPad into a travel alarm (and don't oversleep on the road) with **Alarm Clock HD Pro**. ($0.99/£0.69)

The iPad doesn't come with its own calculator app (unlike the iPhone), but you can fix that easily by getting **Calculator** ($0.99/£0.69). If you need a scientific and engineering calculator, you can't go wrong with sophisticated **PCalc RPN Calculator** ($9.99/£6.99).

Do you ever come across a web page you'd like to read later? You can bookmark those pages, but instead, use **Instapaper** to save them to your iPad and read them at your convenience — even without Internet access. ($4.99/£2.99)

Get weather reports on your iPad wherever you are with **Pocket Weather World HD** ($1.99/£1.49). This app includes more than 60,000 locations worldwide. Or consider the **Weather Channel Max for iPad** (free), which lets you bookmark multiple locations for tracking the weather.

Shopping and Socializing

Amazon Mobile makes it easy (perhaps too easy) to shop on Amazon.com. This well-designed app makes the entire website accessible to you and also lets you track your orders. (Free)

PriceGrabber for iPad helps you find find low prices on just about everything. And, you can read product reviews and compare list prices. (Free)

Look for bargains and hard-to-find items with **eBay for iPad**, the iPad version of the popular shopping website. (Free)

When you're out and about shopping in physical stores, use **Barcode Scanner HD** to scan items and check prices at nearby outlets ($0.99/£0.69).

Sure, you can use the iPad's Notes app for your grocery list, but **Bread and Milk** helps you categorize your purchases, share them, and even plan your route through your grocery store ($1.99/£1.49).

If you use Flickr's photo-sharing service on your computer, why not use **FlickStackr** to bring the same features to your iPad? This is a great app for sharing images with family and friends. ($1.99/£1.49)

The latest social networking craze is Pinterest, and the folks behind the website also have the **Pinterest** app for the iPad so you can pin and view photos when on the go. (Free)

Facebook is the most used social networking service on the planet, and the **Facebook** app keeps you connected and involved when away from your computer. (Free)

Put **Twitter** on your iPad and keep up on the tweets you follow, as well as your own tweets. This app is even handier in iOS 5, because Apple now integrates apps such as Safari and Photos with it. (Free)

Keep up with your instant-messaging buddies via the **AIM** app. (Free)

Retina-Optimized Apps

The third-gen iPad's super–high-resolution Retina display gives apps of all sorts a whole new visual experience. The following is a sampling of apps that take advantage of the new iPad's Retina display.

Business

For businesspeople needing to share data in visual forms, from charts to reports, the **Roambi Flow** service is the perfect tool. Businesses subscribe to the service and get secure access for their employees to the shared business documents, which can contain live data presented in various graphical forms. (Free viewer app; service plan pricing varies)

Skitch for iPad lets you mark up almost anything (photos, web pages, maps, and more) and share the annotated files with anyone via e-mail and Twitter. (Free)

Cooking and Dining

The goodies look even more sumptuous on the new iPad with the **Martha Stewart Cookies** app, which features 90 recipes, videos, baking tips, and more. ($4.99/£2.99)

Education

The **Barefoot World Atlas** helps children explore the world, guided by the BBC's Nick Crane. The app provides a 3D globe to explore, as well as live stats on weather and other facts about each country. ($7.99/£5.49)

Star Walk for iPad is an interactive guide to the heavens. Point your iPad to the sky, and the app shows and labels the stars and constellations above. On the third-gen iPad, more details are visible in the skies, and the images are more realistic. ($4.99/£2.99)

Games

Enjoy a retro space fantasy experience with **Flight Control Rocket**. ($0.99/£0.69)

The popular fantasy combat epic continues in **Infinity Blade II** after the fall of the God King, and it brings you into mesmerizing 3D worlds as you move into the world of the Titans. ($6.99/£4.99)

Become a virtual BMX pro and ride in stunning virtual locations throughout the world with **Touchgrind BMX.** ($4.99/£2.99)

Graphics

Create rich imagery with **SketchBook Pro**. On the third-gen iPad, you get more layers with which to create your artwork. ($4.99/£2.99)

Television

Watch your favorite shows from the ABC-TV network in HD resolution with the **ABC Player** app. (Free)

Your iPad as a Reader

Don't be surprised if you have to answer this question from an inquisitive child someday:

Is it true, Grandpa, that people once read books on paper?

That time may still be a way off, but it somehow doesn't seem as farfetched anymore, especially now that Apple is a major proponent in the burgeoning electronic books revolution.

There are several book-reading apps for the iPad, which turn it into an e-reader, so you don't need a buy a separate device such as the Amazon Kindle or Sony Reader.

Most people love physical books and don't anticipate their imminent demise. But many times, people read a book only once, and the book has no sentimental value as an object. You'll realize how easy it is to let go of such objects the next time you take a long flight and discover that you don't have to make room for a book or two in your limited carry-on luggage — or maybe the next time you don't lug around a thick book on your train commute.

TIP

While lounging around reading, and especially if you're lying down, use the iPad's screen rotation lock feature to stop the iPad from inadvertently rotating the display.

Embracing the Reader

The iPad makes letting go of physical books easy: It's lightweight, it's slim, and it can contain hundreds of books and access thousands of others any time you have an Internet connection — without getting bigger or heavier. The iPad makes a terrific e-reader, supporting color and dazzling special effects in fancier books, and provides a very natural medium from which to read. If you think going from paper books to e-books will somehow feel unnatural, you're in for a pleasant surprise.

Reading books on an iPad is often easier because the iPad

- Weighs less than many hardback and trade paperback books.

- Doesn't cause finger cramping from needing to keep the book open while reading.

- Solves a problem that bedevils older readers — you don't need reading glasses!

It's Many Readers in One

Apple has made a real splash with its free iBooks app and its companion iTunes bookstore. But it's not the only game in town: Amazon.com has made a free iPad app version of its Kindle e-reader. Barnes & Noble has done the same for its Nook. And both — as well as more specialized ebookstores — are available in the App Store. The beauty of the iPad is that you can have any or all of these apps installed, so you have access to multiple online bookstores and e-books — after all, they often don't carry the same items.

*…you have access to **multiple** online bookstores…*

Also nice is that any book you get on your iPad via one of these e-readers can be read on any other device you own that has the same e-reader software. Apple's iBooks, for example, runs on iPads and recent-model iPhones and iPod Touches, so you can start a book on one and finish it on another, all for the price of one copy. The same is true for

Kindle and Nook apps, which are available for iPads, iPod touches, iPhones, Macs, and PCs, as well as for their proprietary e-reader hardware and in some cases for other smartphones such as Android or BlackBerry devices.

Even better, each reader app syncs with all devices you've installed it on, so if you start a book on a Kindle, for example, and open it in the iPad, it picks up where you left off. And any annotations or bookmarks you set are synced across all the devices using the same app as well.

The three reader apps covered in this article are the iBooks, Kindle, and Nook apps. They have similarities and differences, of course, but the iPad's characteristics (for example, the touch screen) facilitate similar functions and operations for these reader apps.

Navigate an E-Book

- Open any reader app and tap a book's cover to open it and begin reading. The book will open to the beginning or to the place you left off reading the last time.

- Place your finger anywhere on a page and flick it to the left to turn to the next page. Flick it to the right to turn to the previous page.

- Tap the right page margin to go to the next page and tap the left page margin to go to the previous page.

- Tap the text (in iBooks) or tap and hold briefly (in the Kindle and Nook apps) to open the onscreen controls. Then tap and drag the slider at the bottom of the page to the right or left to move to another page in the book.

Take the Controls

In the iBooks app, tap the text of an open book to see the onscreen controls. In addition to the page slider at the bottom, you also have controls that give you access to the table of contents, let you adjust the screen's display (brightness, font, text size, and page color), and give you searching and bookmarking options.

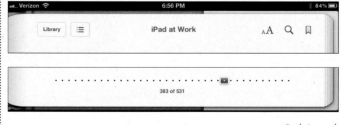

iBooks' controls

DUMMIES

In the Kindle app, you tap the open book's page and hold briefly to see the onscreen controls. Unlike the iBooks app, you find most of the controls at the bottom of the page. They include a page slider, Search and Bookmark tools, a Jump control (to specify a particular location in the book to jump to), and a Sync with Amazon control. At the top, the Home control takes you back to the list of available books.

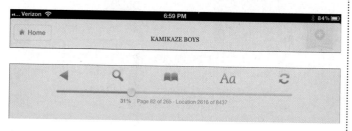

The Kindle app's controls

Search Inside or Out

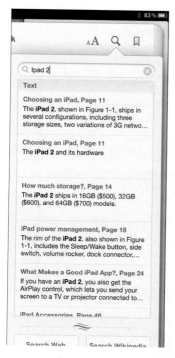

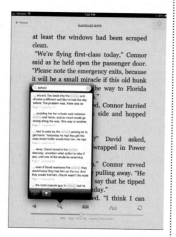

iBooks (left) and Kindle (right)

- All the reader apps have some kind of search function. In the iBooks app, tap the Search button (the magnifying glass icon) and tap again in the Search box that opens using the onscreen keyboard. Tap Search when you're done. The Search box expands to include a list of all occurrences of your search phrase in the book. (You may need to scroll down to see them all.) Tap a result to jump to its page. Or tap outside the Search dialog box to close it and stay on the current page.

- In the iBooks app (as well as the Kindle and Nook apps), you can also search for a word or phrase on Google or the Wikipedia online encyclopedia. Just use the buttons at the bottom of the iBooks search results.

Bookmark, Highlight, and Make Notes

Moving around to a particular location on the iPad is almost as simple as moving around a real book, and e-readers kindly return you to the last page you were reading when you closed a book. Still, occasionally you want to somehow mark or annotate a specific page or text selection.

- **Bookmark a page:** In the iBooks app, simply tap any text on a page; the Bookmark button appears (along with the Display and Search buttons) at the upper right of the screen. Tap the Bookmark button to set a bookmark (which appears as a red ribbon) for that page. The process is similar for the Kindle: You just tap and hold for the onscreen controls and tap the Bookmark icon, which looks like a ribbon with a + sign.

- **Highlight a passage:** Just as you might by using a yellow marker in a printed textbook — it's also easy to do. In the iBooks, Kindle, and Nook apps, you can select a word or group of words and tap the Highlight control that appears. What you've selected then shows up with a yellow background.

- **Add your own note to a passage:** Again, the process is similar on the iBooks and Kindle apps. Select the text and tap the Note button that appears above your selection. Use the onscreen keyboard to type your note in the sticky note or window that comes up. In iBooks, tap outside the note to close it; in the Kindle app, tap Save. The text gets a colored background (by default, yellow), and a sticky note icon appears. Tap the note to open it to read it. In the Nook app, you select the text, tap Add Notes, and use the onscreen keyboard to type your note in the window that appears. Then tap Save.

"We're flying fi[Note Highlight Share] Connor said as he held open the passenger door. "Please note the emergency exits, because it will be a small miracle if this old hunk

"Please note the emergency exits, because it will be a small of junk makes it without breaking
Once David was seated, Connor hurried

Cars don't really have these, of course. It's a metaphor. [Save]

Annotating in the Kindle app

When you want to find your bookmark, highlighted text, or notes again, tap the Table of Contents button and then Bookmarks in the iBooks app. The resulting Bookmarks pane shows them all. Tap an entry to return to that spot in the book. In the Kindle app, tap and hold to get the onscreen controls. Then tap the Bookmarks button to open the Go To menu. Tap My Notes & Marks to get a list of bookmarks, highlights, and annotations; then tap the one you want to go to. Similarly, in the Nook app, tap the Contents button at the top of the screen and then, in the pop-over that appears, tap Annotations to see your notes or Bookmarks to see your bookmarked pages.

Adjust the Interface

The various reader apps let you make the screen brighter or dimmer per your visual preference (or to save on power by dimming the screen on a flight or other location without power). The apps have a Brightness slider that you adjust to change the screen brightness. I find that setting the screen to about 59 to 65 percent brightness makes for a more paper-like reading experience that is easy on the eyes.

Each app also gives you a way to adjust the style and size of the typeface, and in some cases, text spacing and justification, as well as the color of the page, text, highlights, and so on. In the Nook app, you can actually save the settings you make as a theme.

iBooks app

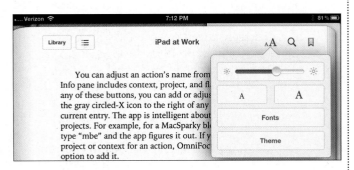

Adjust screen brightness and type size, choose a type style, and change the page color.

Kindle app

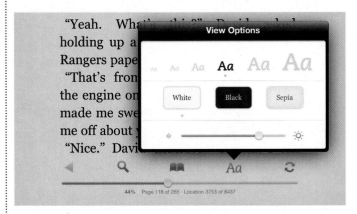

Choose one of six text sizes and one of three colors.

Nook app

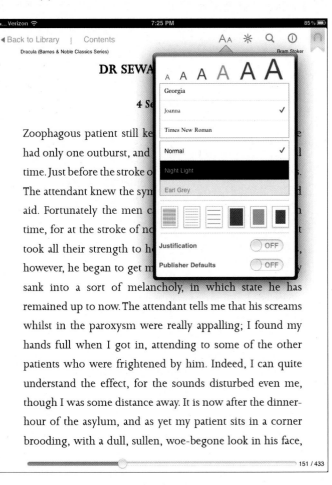

Change text sizes, line spacing, justification, type style, and various colors.

Manage an E-Book Library

The iBooks app gives you some control over how its Library window displays:

✔ **Changing the view:** If you'd prefer to view a list than see your books on a bookshelf, tap the List button (with three lines) in the upper right of the screen. You can sort the list by title, author, or category, or you can rearrange where books appear on the bookshelf. To return to the bookshelf view, tap the Bookshelf button (with four squares).

✔ **Rearranging books on the bookshelf:** To perform this feat, make sure the app is showing the bookshelf view. Then drag a book to a new location in the bookshelf — you need to tap and hold on the book briefly before you can drag it.

✔ **Removing a book from the bookshelf:** In the list view, tap Edit and then tap the red circle with the minus sign to the left of the book title you want to remove. Then tap Delete. In the bookshelf view, tap Edit and then tap the black circle with the white X that appears in the upper-left corner of a book cover. Then tap Delete.

The Kindle app shows your current books on its Home screen. The default view is the cover view, but there's also a list view.

✔ **Switch among the views** by using the Cover/List toggle button at the bottom left of the screen. You can also change how the books are sorted by clicking the Sort button to its right; your options are Recent, Title, and Author.

✔ **Manage books from the Home screen** when you want to keep that screen uncluttered or to show only unread books there. To see just books on the iPad, tap the Device button at the bottom of the screen; tap Cloud to see all purchased books. To move a book to the device, tap and hold it in Cloud view and then choose Download from the contextual menu that appears. To remove a book from the Device view, tap and hold it, and then choose Remove from Device from the contextual menu that appears.

To add ePub, Office, and PDF documents to the Kindle app, mail them to your Kindle address, which is usually something like jsmith@kindle.com.

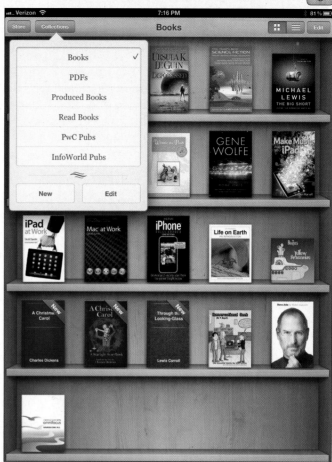

The Nook app lets you manage your library of books from the app's Home screen. At the top of the screen, you see the management controls for your books. By default, you see the covers arranged in a grid.

- ✔ **Adjust your view of content:** The Nook app shows its content only as a grid of covers; you can't get to a list view. But you can use the All Items pop-up menu to change the view to just books, just magazines, just newspapers, archived content, and of course all items. The Most Recent pop-up menu lets you sort by title or author, and the Search box lets you search your library.

- ✔ **Manage your book storage:** Tap and hold a book cover to get a detail screen that includes two key buttons: Archive (for books you've read and maybe don't want on your home screen) and Delete. If you tap Delete, you get a pop-up menu with three options: Cancel, Remove from Device, and Delete Permanently. If you choose Remove from Device, the book's cover remains in the Nook app but has a Download button added; you need to tap that button to reload the book onto your iPad.

Using PDFs and ePubs with iBooks

You may have noticed the Collections button in the iBooks library. By default, iBooks shows the Books pane, which contains any books you get from the iTunes bookstore. But iBooks can also hold PDF files and ePub-formatted documents that you sync to it via iTunes. Any PDFs are accessed by tapping the Collections button, which presents a separate library of PDF documents. (ePubs reside in the Books pane by default.)

You can also create your own folders for books, PDFs, and ePubs using the controls in the Collections dialog box. Move library items among them by tapping Edit, selecting the items, tapping Move, and then choosing the collection to place them in. To get a PDF or an ePub document into iBooks, drag the file on your computer on to the iTunes Library on the same computer and then sync your iPad to that computer.

Any ePubs you want to import via iTunes must be *DRM*-free, which means they are free of digital rights restrictions.

When you're reading PDFs, iBooks offers you different options than for ePubs and e-books. You can search PDF documents and bookmark their pages just as you would a book. You can move from page to page by sliding to the left or right, and you can scroll through their pages using the bar at the bottom of the screen. But you can't tap the page margin to move to the next or previous page. You can't add highlights or annotations, either. Nor can you change the text display. But you can zoom in and out using the standard iPad pinch and expand gestures.

Buying Books

IN THIS ARTICLE

- *Buying online through Safari*
- *Buying through the app's store*

Buying books works a little differently for each of the reader apps. The source varies: You buy books from Apple via the iTunes bookstore on your iPad's iBooks app or via iTunes on your computer, but you buy books from Amazon.com or Barnes & Noble from their websites. In each case, you need to set up an account of some sort so you can pay for your purchases.

When buying through the iBooks app, a Featured pane presents Apple's recommendations, the NY Times pane shows *The New York Times* best-sellers list, and the Top Charts pane present the iTunes bookstore's top sellers' list. The Categories pane lets you explore specific genres. The Browse pane lets you view books by their authors. The Purchased pane shows you what you've bought, and lets you re-download previous purchases not on your iPad. You'll find that navigating the iTunes bookstore is very much like navigating through the iTunes Store.

TIP

In the iBooks app, you can download free samples before you buy. You get to read several pages of the book to see whether it appeals to you, and it doesn't cost you a dime! Look for the Get Sample button when you view details about a book. Amazon.com and Barnes & Noble also offer samples at their websites that you can send to your iPad.

REMEMBER

If you have an iTunes Gift Card you want to use to pay for your purchases, scroll to the bottom of the screen and tap Redeem; then enter the card's code and tap Redeem. Any books you buy are first charged against your current gift card balance and then against the credit card associated with your iTunes account.

Buying for iBooks

Buying books for the iBooks app requires that you have an iTunes account. The process is similar on the iPad's iTunes bookstore and on iTunes on your computer, though some controls may be in different locations:

① In the iBooks library, tap the Store button. The iBookstore opens.

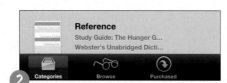

② Browse books in the panes you get via the Featured, NY Times, Top Charts, Categories, and Browse buttons — or type a term in the Search box to find a book by name, subject, or author. In the Browse pane, find books by author or, if you go to the Category pane, by category.

③ When you find a book you want to buy, tap its price (sometimes free); then tap Buy Book (or Get Book) to confirm the purchase. You may need to enter your iTunes password; do so and tap OK. The book downloads to your library immediately.

Buying for Kindle

To buy books for the Kindle app, you do so through the Amazon.com website, either from a computer or from your iPad's Safari browser. You of course need to have an account set up at Amazon.com so it can charge your purchases.

When you complete a purchase, you choose a device to send the book to from the Deliver To pop-up menu. When you first used the Kindle app, you registered your iPad with Amazon.com, so it appears as a Deliver To option. If you choose your iPad here, the book is uploaded to the Kindle app's Home screen the next time the iPad is connected to the Internet. If you sent the book to a different device, you see it in the Archived Items list in the iPad's Kindle app; tap the book in that list to download it to the iPad.

Buying for Nook

Buying books for the Nook is an activity that takes place on the Barnes & Noble website, www.bn.com. You can go there from your computer or iPad browser. You buy a book the usual way, which adds it to the Nook app's Home screen on your iPad the next time you open the Nook app and have an active Internet connection. Tap Download to transfer the book to your iPad.

Introducing the Multi-Touch E-Book

T he iBooks 2.0 app on an iPad lets you read a special type of e-book available for no other device or computer, what Apple calls a Multi-Touch e-book produced in the free iBooks Author software for the Mac. Multi-Touch e-books can have embedded videos, 3D objects, chapter review quizzes, interactive annotated images, photo galleries, slideshows, and a variety of other types of dynamic content.

They also can have glossaries and let you add detailed notes; both capabilities reflect Apple's initial focus of Multi-Touch e-books as a platform for educational material. At the iBookstore, you can find such educational titles in the Textbook section. But the Multi-Touch format is available for books in any topic, so expect to see cookbooks, travel guides, and other books take advantage of it as well.

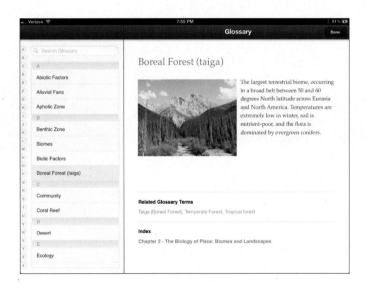

Multi-Touch e-books look and work differently in portrait orientation than landscape orientation. Read the e-book in landscape orientation to get a more traditional print-book layout style.

Reading Periodicals

The iPad is a great reader for more than books, of course: It makes it easy to keep up with magazines, newspapers, and more. You can read many periodicals on the web via the Safari browser, of course, but that doesn't give you the full iPad experience. For that, you want apps — and there are plenty of them.

Many take full advantage of the iPad to provide a great reading experience. The *Economist, Wall Street Journal, Le Monde, USA Today, San Francisco Chronicle,* and *New York Times* are all great examples of print periodicals whose iPad editions are easy to use on the iPad, reflowing the layouts as your iPad's orientation changes, including videos and other elements print can't handle, and allowing for larger text sizes for people who hate wearing reading glasses. The Reuters and BBC news services' apps likewise are well designed for the iPad. (Most also have good iPhone versions.)

By contrast, some magazine apps such as the *National Geographic* give you essentially just a PDF-like static view of a magazine's pages, and often require scrolling and zooming to read the text.

Many magazines and newspapers have apps that let you read individual issues (either paid for individually through the app or via a subscription you get through the app or by entering a code, such as the subscriber code on the mailing label of the print edition). Like all apps, you get the periodicals' apps at the App Store.

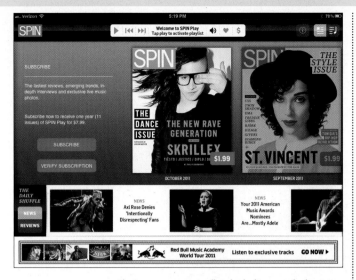

The Spin magazine app sells individual issues and subscriptions.

The Newsstand app with three active subscriptions

The Newsstand section of the App Store

TIP

Many periodicals' apps don't support Newsstand, so they won't appear in its rack of publications; instead, they're on your Home screen along with your other apps. So you might want to place them near the Newsstand app so your reading materials are in close proximity.

iOS 5 brings in an app called Newsstand that collects compatible periodicals apps into one place, so you can see your "rack" of publications in one place, including those which have new issues. Click a periodical within Newsstand to open its app and get the latest edition. Newsstand also gives you the Store button that opens the App Store's Newsstand section of periodicals apps.

You can also find apps such as Zinio that act like Newsstand in that they let you view issues of multiple periodicals. And Amazon.com lets you get magazine and newspaper subscriptions through its Kindle app.

Yet another way to read on the iPad is through a "build your own magazine" app such as Zite or Flipbook. These apps use your preferences — usually determined by examining your Twitter, Facebook, and other social media accounts — to pull together relevant content from the web into a magazine-like package that continuously updates itself.

Routine Upkeep

A pple is known for its high quality products, so you rarely have to worry about your iPad or other Apple product failing due to a quality issue. And should that rare event happen, Apple's customer support will arrange for a replacement or repair as long as the device is under warranty. You can call Apple, go to its website, or go to an Apple Store for help.

Of course, it's possible to damage your iPad: You can crack the screen by dropping it or striking it forcefully, for example. You can insert inappropriate objects into one of its ports or get them wet, damaging the port and perhaps some internal circuitry. You do need to treat an iPad with care, just as you would any other piece of computer equipment.

Photo by Ingall W. Bull III

Apple's iPad Case is one of many options to protect your original iPad, while the Smart Cover is an option for your third-gen iPad or iPad 2.

A Case for Protection

Dozens and dozens of sleeves and cases are available, so it's easy to find the one that's right for you and your specific criteria. A prime function of a case is to protect the iPad itself by shielding it from scratches, blows, and spills. Sure, they also can personalize your iPad, make it easier to carry (by making it less slippery), and/or act as a riser — but any case you buy should also help shield your iPad from outside elements.

Protective cases come in two basic types: sleeves (also called skins) and portfolios. A *sleeve* envelopes the iPad but leaves its screen open for use. A *portfolio* holds the iPad but usually has a fold-over cover or a portfolio-like design so the screen can be protected. A Portfolio may also let you carry paper, styli, and the like as well. Its cover may also fold to let it act a riser. The third-gen iPad and the iPad 2 support magnetically attached covers, as well.

Apple's iPad Case is a great folder-style case for your iPad 1: Its texture is quite grippable, it raises the iPad to an angle perfect for typing, and it's not bulky. But it interferes with Apple's own iPad docks and doesn't let you stand the iPad up for video viewing. The Apple Smart Cover for the third-gen iPad and the iPad 2, an ingenious cover, is both grippable and handy for standing the iPad in several poses.

Removing Fingerprints

If you've been using your iPad at all, you know (despite Apple's claim about fingerprint-resistant screens) that iPads are fingerprint magnets. Here are some tips on how to clean your iPad screen:

- You can get most fingerprints off with a dry, soft cloth such as the one you use to clean your eyeglasses or camera lenses, or use a dry cleaning tissue that is lint- and chemical-free.

- If you want to get the surface even cleaner, you can use a soft cloth that has been *slightly* dampened. Again, make sure whatever cloth material you use is free of lint. But be careful: You don't want any liquid to get into your iPad as that could damage its electronics. Be sure to turn off the iPad and unplug any cables from it before cleaning the screen with a moistened cloth. And take care not to get much moisture around the edges of the screen where it could seep into the unit.

- *Never* use any household cleaners on your iPad screen. They can degrade the coating that keeps the screen from absorbing oil from your fingers.

- *Never* use premoistened lens-cleaning tissues to clean your screen. Most of these wipes contain alcohol, which can damage the coating.

Recharging Your iPad

Your iPad can run as long as 12 hours on a full charge — most people get 10 to 11 hours of active usage. And if it's not in use, it goes to sleep after a few minutes, which lengthens the times between recharges considerably. But when you do need to recharge your iPad, it can take six or so hours to go from depleted to fully charged. If you don't have that long, recharge the iPad for about 20 minutes to get about 45 minutes of active usage.

- When recharging your iPad, *don't* plug the iPad's dock connector-to-USB cable into a USB port on your keyboard, monitor, or USB hub. They likely don't have the full 10 watts of power necessary to charge the iPad. (They work with iPhones and other devices because those use just 5 watts or less.)

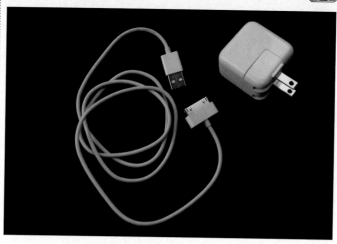

The 10-watt power supply that comes with the iPad is your safest bet for recharging.

- If you have a newer computer, its built-in USB ports may provide sufficient power. (If not, your iPad will sync just fine; it just won't recharge.) So use the power cord that came with your iPad.

- If the iPad's status bar says *Not Charging* next to the battery icon at the top of the screen, that means whatever you've plugged it into isn't delivering the necessary 10 watts of power.

Your iPad's battery is sealed in the unit, so you can't replace it as you can with a laptop or cellphone battery when it won't recharge fully. An authorized repair shop can replace the battery if it's out of warranty, for about $100. Contact Apple to replace a problematic battery if the iPad is under warranty.

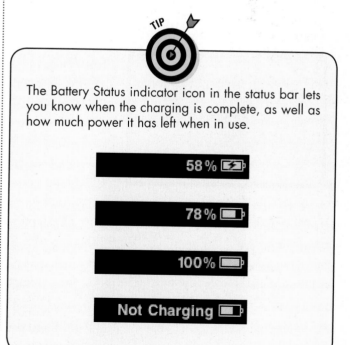

The Battery Status indicator icon in the status bar lets you know when the charging is complete, as well as how much power it has left when in use.

58%
78%
100%
Not Charging

Securing Access to Your iPad

Your iPad can contain a lot of sensitive information: your e-mail, bookmarked websites, and even documents. Plus if you have a Wi-Fi/cellular model, someone who borrows your iPad without permission could run through your cellular data service's bucket of bytes. The iPad can require a passcode be entered to allow access, and it's a good idea to set such a passcode. When set, the passcode must be entered to use the iPad after it has been turned off, restarted, or gone to sleep. You can also set the iPad to require the passcode after a specified period of inactivity. If you use your iPad to connect to your office e-mail using a Microsoft Exchange server or the corporate Gmail edition, your network administrator can force

The iPad can require a passcode...and it's a good idea

your iPad to require a passcode and specify the period of inactivity that requires the passcode to be entered. (You can also lock or wipe your iPad yourself using the Find My iPad app on a Mac, another iOS device, or from iCloud.com.) The administrator can also disable or set other access-related controls, such as the Erase Data and Auto-Lock controls. So if you didn't set a passcode requirement for your iPad, maybe your network administrator did. The passcode is almost always the same as your passcode to access the office e-mail from your computer. Don't worry if the iPad is locked. It still receives notification alerts, and you can adjust its volume with the rocker switch on the iPad's side.

Set the passcode in the Settings app:

1 Open the General pane by tapping General in the Sidebar. Tap Passcode Lock. If no passcode had been previously set, enter one as prompted; then tap Done. Enter the passcode again to confirm it and tap Done.

2 If a passcode was previously set, you must enter it to prove you should have access. Tap Change Passcode. Enter your current password and tap Done. You're then asked to enter the new passcode.

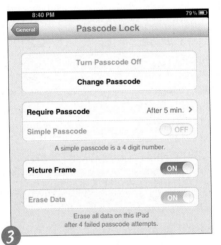

3 Set other related options:

- Tap Require Passcode to choose the period of inactivity that requires the iPad to ask for a passcode for continued usage.

- (Optional) Slide the Picture Frame switch to Off if you don't want to have the iPad act as a picture frame when locked. (The Picture Frame button isn't on the locked-iPad screen in this case.)

- (Optional) Slide the Erase Data switch to On if you want the iPad to wipe all its data after eight failed attempts to enter a correct password. (Your computer's iTunes will have all apps and data from the last sync. And your iCloud or e-mail server may still contain at least some of your e-mails.)

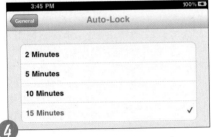

4 Tap General to return to the General pane. Optionally, tap Auto-Lock to specify after how much inactivity the iPad locks itself.

TIP

You can use the Auto-Lock with the Passcode Lock setting. For example, you might set Passcode Lock to 15 minutes and Auto-Lock to 2 minutes. In that case, after 2 minutes, the iPad screen locks, so someone has to slide the Unlock slider to make the screen visible — this can help keep your screen's display private without requiring a password to continue working. After 15 minutes, a passcode is required.

Setting VPN access

Many businesses secure access to their networks and files by using something called a virtual private network (VPN). To access data protected via VPN, you need to set the iPad to access that VPN. You need the proper access information from your company, but the process is simple:

1. In the Settings app's General pane, tap Network to open the Network pane.

2. Tap VPN. In the VPN pane that appears, tap Add VPN Configuration.

3. The Add Configuration dialog box appears. Tap the type of VPN you use — L2TP, PPTP, or IPSec — then complete the settings as provided by your company.

4. Click Save.

5. The iPad will try to verify the VPN settings by connecting (so you should have an active Internet connection). You'll likely have to enter a password as part of that process. If successful, the VPN connection is saved in the VPN pane.

To use the VPN, slide the VPN switch to On in the Settings app's Sidebar. To edit a VPN configuration, tap Network from the Sidebar and then tap VPN in the Network pane to open the VPN pane. Tap the saved VPN configuration to open a dialog box with settings you can edit as needed.

Using the iPhone Configuration Utility, Apple Configurator, or a mobile management tool, your company can send you an e-mail attachment or web link that sets up the VPN for you; some tools can even automatically set up the VPN without your intervention.

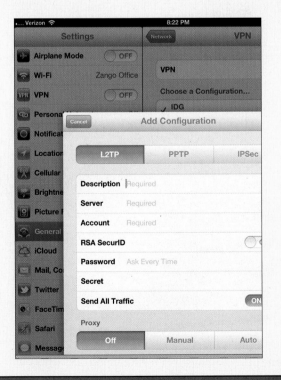

Find a Lost or Stolen iPad

To sign up for the Find My iPad service, go to the Settings app's iCloud pane and set the Find My iPad switch to On. (If you don't have an iCloud account, you can set one up in this pane first. You also log into your account from this pane.)

Should you lose your iPad, you can go to **www.icloud.com** from another computer or device, sign in, and see whether your iPad's location is available, and/or remote-wipe its contents. You can also use the Find iPhone, Find iPad, or Find iPod app on another device to find and lock or wipe your iPad; just sign in using your iCloud credentials.

*The Find My iPad service is **free**.*

Enabling the Find My iPad feature

Using the Find iPad/iPhone/iPod app (here, on an iPhone)

Customizing the Interface

The iPad provides a great deal of user-interface customization, so you can make it work the way you need or want it to. For example, you get control over volume, what sounds accompany iPad functions, the time zone for your calendar, and defaults for using your onscreen keyboards. Such settings generally work across the iPad's apps, affecting most functions on the iPad.

As you might expect, the Settings app is where you can adjust these settings. Most are accessed via the General pane, but not all. To go to the General pane, tap General in the Settings app's left pane (called its Sidebar).

Setting Typing Defaults

Tap Keyboard in the General pane to control the iPad's typing behavior. You have eight options, shown in the table on the next page.

Option	Controls	What It Does
Auto-Capitalization	On/Off	When On, corrects capitalization errors for known proper names and any lowercase word that follows a period (.), question mark (?), or exclamation mark (!).
Auto-Correction	On/Off	When On, corrects spelling errors as you type. Corrections are made when you tap the spacebar or a punctuation character. Override a correction before the iPad makes it by tapping the X icon that appears to the right of its suggestion.
Check Spelling	On/Off	When On, flags possible spelling errors in compatible applications by placing a red squiggly line beneath suspect words.
Enable Caps Lock	On/Off	When On, lets you double-tap the Shift key to turn on caps lock. Tap Shift again to return to lowercase.
"." Shortcut	On/Off	When On, replaces two consecutive spaces with a period and a space.
International Keyboards	Add New Keyboard	Manage additional onscreen keyboards for other languages. Tap Add New Keyboard to add a keyboard in a language of your choice. You can add several, one at a time.
International Keyboards	Edit	With at least two keyboards enabled, tap Edit to rearrange their order or delete unwanted keyboards.
Add New Shortcut	Edit	Enter a shortcut that when typed in any app is replaced by the longer text you specify. You can set up multiple such shortcuts. (This is new to iOS 5.)

Getting Sound Reinforcement

Getting audio feedback can make a huge difference when you're working on the iPad, as it lets you know you did what you intended. Tap Sounds in the Settings app's General pane to set the audio feedback.

The Sounds pane has two sections. In the top section, you use the volume slider to set the overall audio level for music and other sounds played by the iPad. If you don't want a change in volume made with the iPad's physical rocker switch to affect alerts and ringers, set the Change with Buttons switch to Off, so these tones are always audible.

The second section lets you set the specific ringer sound (or disable the ringer) for several kinds of ringers: phone and calling apps (the Ringtone control), text messages (the Text Tone control), e-mails received, e-mails sent, tweets,

calendar alerts, and reminder alerts. (These customizable ringers are new to iOS 5.) You can also turn off the sound made when the iPad is locked and when you tap a keyboard key.

Changing with the Time Zones . . .

The iPad has a built-in calendar and clock, which you can set using the Date & Time controls in the Settings app's General pane:

- **24-Hour Time:** Set this to On if you want time to display in military or European style, such as 15:00 rather than 3:00 PM.

- **Set Automatically:** Set this to On if you want the iPad to find out the current date and time automatically. (It needs an active Internet connection.) If you set this to On, the Time Zone control is inaccessible and the Set Date & Time control disappears.

- **Time Zone:** Tap this to enter the name of a city whose time zone you want this iPad to use.

- **Set Date & Time:** Tap this to manually enter a date and time.

. . . Or Not

When you travel, you probably want your iPad to display time in the local time zone. But you may want your calendar to stay in your home time zone. That can make sense if you're scheduling events with people back home and want to be using their time zone when setting up appointments. The iPad lets you keep your calendar in your home time zone — or for that matter, in any specific time zone — regardless of what the local time zone happens to be.

To specify that the iPad's Calendar app uses a specific time zone, tap Mail, Contacts, Calendars in the Settings app's Sidebar. Scroll to the bottom of the pane and tap Time Zone Support. In the Time Zone Support pane that appears, slide the Time Zone Support switch to On; then tap the Time Zone control to set the city whose time zone you want the Calendar app to use.

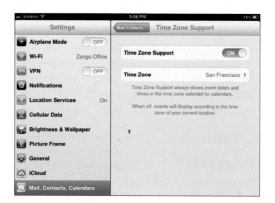

Connecting Bluetooth Devices

The iPad supports the Bluetooth short-range wireless technology that lets you connect devices to it without cables. The iPad supports three types of Bluetooth devices: keyboards, headphones and headsets, and Braille readers. You can also use Bluetooth to communicate with other iPads and computers if you have peer-to-peer apps installed on the devices you want to connect; such apps allow for data sharing.

By default, Bluetooth is turned off on your iPad because it can drain your battery in just a few hours. To turn it on, tap Bluetooth in the Settings app's General pane and then slide the Bluetooth switch to On. Any available and compatible Bluetooth devices display in the Bluetooth pane. Tap a device's name to connect to it; you may get a pairing request, where you have to enter a code that indicates you have permission to connect to the device.

Using Notifications

iOS 5 brings with it more ways for the iPad to get your attention when needed. In the Notifications pane of the Settings app, you can set which apps may send you notifications and how. Any app in the Notifications Center section will leave its alerts for you in the pull-down alerts tray called the Notification Center.

To see the Notification Center, tap and pull down from the top of the screen (where the time displays) in any app. Tap a notification to open it up in its app.

In the Notifications pane, tap an app's name to specify how it notifies you. Set Notification Setting to On to have it appear in the Notification Center, and use the Show control to specify the maximum number of alerts for that app that are displayed.

FOR DUMMIES

You can also set three other alerts:

✔ **Alert Style:** This sets how alerts are displayed: not at all, in a temporary banner at the top of the screen, or as an alert dialog box in the middle of the screen.

✔ **Badge App Icon:** If set to On, this places a red circle on the app's Home screen icon indicating how many alerts are awaiting you for that app.

✔ **View in Lock Screen:** If set to On, this displays any notifications for that app in your lock screen when the iPad is locked. You can slide the app's icon in the lock screen to unlock the iPad and see the alert in the app.

Who am I?

You can have iOS auto-fill some information in the Mail, Contacts, Calendars pane and in other apps if you tell it who you are. To do that, go to the Mail, Contacts, Calendars pane of the Settings app and then tap My Info in the Contacts section. Select your name from the list of contacts. Now your iPad knows who you are.

Going International

The iPad is a multilingual device. If you're also multilingual, you can have the iPad use multiple languages, as well as choose your desired language for the user interface, even if it's not the standard language for the country where you bought the iPad. These controls are in the General pane, in which you tap International to open the International pane.

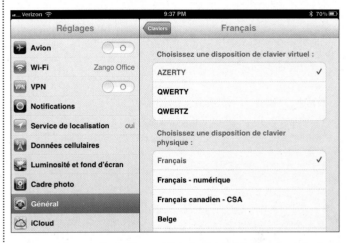

The Settings app with the iPad's default language changed to French

✔ **Interface language:** Tap Language to choose the default language; the iPad supports 34 languages (including some regional variations such as both American and British English, and both European and Brazilian Portuguese). Tap the desired language and then tap Done.

✔ **Language keyboards:** Tap Keyboards to change the default onscreen keyboard's display to be that of another language or to add additional languages' keyboards. (If you add language keyboards, the onscreen keyboard will have a key with a globe icon on it that lets you switch keyboards.)

In the Keyboards pane, tap the language button (it probably says *English*, but if you've set up other languages, you get a button for each) at the top of the screen to change the default keyboard settings. You have these choices:

✔ **Onscreen keyboard arrangement:** In the Software Keyboard & Layout section, select QWERTY, AZERTY, or QWERTZ to choose the keyboard layout for the iPad's onscreen keyboard.

✔ **Physical keyboard:** In the Hardware Keyboard & Layout section, select the type of physical keyboard you are using with the iPad.

In the Keyboards pane, tap Add New Keyboard to make additional language keyboards available to the iPad's onscreen keyboard. There are 56 keyboard layouts available to choose from (even Cherokee!).

Setting Accessibility Options

The iPad lets you customize the user interface to work better if you have a visual or hearing disability. Most of these options are in the General pane of the Settings app; tap Accessibility to see the options.

TIP

You can also enable the Accessibility controls in iTunes on your computer. With your iPad connected and selected in the iTunes Sidebar's Devices list, go to the Summary pane, scroll to the bottom, and then click Universal Access.

VoiceOver

This screen reader describes aloud what's on the screen. It can read e-mail messages, web pages, and more. With VoiceOver active, you tap an item on the screen to select it. VoiceOver then places a black rectangle around it and either speaks the item's name or describes an item. For example, if you tap, say, Brightness & Wallpaper in the Settings app, the VoiceOver voice speaks the words "Brightness & Wallpaper button." VoiceOver even lets you know when you change the iPad's orientation to landscape or portrait, as well as when your screen is locked or unlocked.

Tap VoiceOver to set its behavior with these controls:

- Slide the VoiceOver switch to On to enable VoiceOver. Note that you need to double-tap buttons to activate them because a single tap now makes the iPad read the button's label.

- Slide the Speak Hints slider to On to have the iPad provide instructions on what to do next (where it can), along the lines of "double-tap to open."

- Drag the Speaking Rate slider to speed up or slow down the voice.

- Tap Typing Feedback to tell the iPad what to say when you're typing: each character as you type it, the words only (after you tap a space or a punctuation character), both, or none.

- Slide the Use Phonetics switch to Off to disable the use of words such as *alpha* and *bravo* to describe single characters such as A and B being pressed. Note that these words are used only if you pause after tapping a character, as an extra confirmation of what you pressed.

- Slide the Pitch Change switch to Off to disable the use of a lower pitch to indicate deleted text.

Zoom

The Zoom feature, if turned on, offers a screen magnifier for those who are visually impaired. To zoom by 200 percent, double-tap the screen with *three* fingers. Drag three fingers to move around the screen. To increase magnification, use three fingers to tap and drag up. Tap with three fingers and drag down to decrease magnification.

Note that when magnified, the characters on the screen aren't as crisp, and you can't display as much in a single view.

Large Text

This control lets you set the text size in the Calendar, Contacts, Mail, Messages, and Notes apps, to make items such as e-mails more readable.

White on Black

If this control is set to On, the colors on the iPad are reversed to provide a higher contrast for people with poor eyesight. The screen resembles a film negative.

Speak Selection

Turn this on to add Speak and Pause options to the contextual menus when you select text in applications such as Mail, Notes, and Safari, so your iPad can read the selected text aloud to you.

Speak Auto-Text

When this control is set to On, the iPad automatically speaks autocorrections and capitalizations.

Mono Audio

If you suffer hearing loss in one ear, turn this control to On so the iPad combines the right and left audio channels so both are heard in each earbud of any headset you plug in. (This control does not affect the iPad's built-in speaker, which is not stereo.)

Assistive Touch

Tap this option to open a pane where you can enable the new capability in iOS 5 to access gestures through menus rather than by performing the gestures yourself. When you set the Assistive Touch switch to On, a circle button appears at the bottom right of all iPad screens. Tap it to get a pictorial menu of gestures; that menu has submenus for additional gestures.

You can also create your own gestures in the Custom Gestures section. Tap Create New Gesture and then do the gesture on the screen. Save it and name it; the gesture will appear in the Favorites pictorial menu of the Assistive Gestures menu. Note that you cannot specify an action for a custom gesture, so it should be something you do repeatedly in an app, either one of its special gestures or an action like flipping through elements in a web page in a common order.

  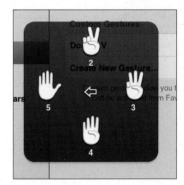

Triple-Click Home

Use the Triple-Click Home feature to specify what happens when you triple-press the Home button: Turn VoiceOver on or off, switch between black-on-white and white-on-black display, or ask what to do. If you choose Ask, your options when triple-pressing Home include toggling VoiceOver, toggling White on Black, and toggling Zoom. You can also select Off to disable triple-pressing.

Closed Captioning

In the Video pane of the Settings app (tap Video in the Sidebar), you can turn on closed-captioning subtitles for a movie or video in which they are available. To do so, slide the Close Captioning switch to On.

Large text in e-mail

If you want to have just your e-mail's text be large, and not affect the text size in the other applications that the Accessibility pane's Large Text Size option affects, go instead to the Mail, Contacts, Calendars pane and set the desired message text size by tapping the Minimum Font Size option in the Mail section.

Backing Up and Restoring Your iPad

Sometimes, bad things happen to electronic devices, and an iPad is no exception. Whether your iPad is lost, stolen, damaged, or loses its data, you want to be able to recover what you had on the iPad and restore it on that iPad or on a new one so you can keep iPadding.

Apple makes it easy to back up your iPad, so there's no excuse not to. Here are the basic mechanisms available:

✔ **iTunes automatic backup:** The iPad automatically syncs with iTunes daily, but only if your iPad is plugged in to a power source and connected to a Wi-Fi network, and only if your computer is running, connected to a network that in turn is connected to the Wi-Fi network, has iTunes running, and has the Back Up to This Computer option selected in the Summary pane for that iPad. To encrypt the data — so a password is needed to restore it — select the Encrypt Backup option.

Syncing to iTunes over Wi-Fi (top). iCloud provides a backup option (bottom).

✔ **iTunes manual backup:** When you connect your iPad to iTunes via its cable, the Sync button appears at the bottom right of the screen. Click it to back up your iPad's data and settings to your computer. On the iPad, if both your iPad and computer are connected to the same network (and iTunes is running on your computer), you can wirelessly sync the iPad by going to the Settings app's General pane, tapping iTunes Wi-Fi Sync to open its pane, and then tapping Sync Now. You can see the date and time of your last backup in the iTunes Wi-Fi Sync pane.

✓ **iCloud backup:** You can also turn on iCloud backup, either in iTunes (in the Summary pane for the iPad) or in the Settings app on the iPad. (Go to the iCloud pane and then tap Storage & Backup.) If enabled, your iPad backs up to iCloud whenever it's locked, plugged in to a power source, and connected to the Internet via Wi-Fi.

The backup options in iTunes

iCloud backup backs up only the Photos app's Camera Roll album, your settings, your documents, and your account information. Your apps and any music, e-books, or videos purchased via iTunes are always kept at Apple's servers, so although they aren't backed up to iCloud, they'll be redownloaded to your iPad if you're signed in to the Apple Store. (Go to the Store pane of the Settings app to do so.) Everything is backed up to iTunes if you choose iTunes backup, which means your purchases don't have to be redownloaded but instead are copied back from your computer.

Updating iOS

Apple doesn't stand still, and neither does the iOS operating system that lets the iPad work its magic. Therefore, a few times per year, Apple typically releases updates to iOS to fix issues in the operating system and add new capabilities. But unless you install them on your iPad, you can't take advantage of the changes.

With iOS 5, Apple made it easy to update iOS. It's automatic. When a new iOS version is available, you'll get an alert on your iPad asking if you want to install it — if you're on a Wi-Fi network. You'll also get a notice when you connect your iPad to iTunes via the USB-to-30-pin cable.

You can also force the issue on both your iPad and in iTunes (if you told the iPad not to update iOS when it first alerted you):

✓ **On the iPad:** In the Settings app, go to the General pane and tap Software to see if there's an available update. If so, tap the Download and Install button to begin the process.

✓ **In iTunes:** Connect your iPad via its cable and click your iPad's name in the Sidebar's Devices list. Click the Check for Update button; if an update is available, you're asked whether you want to back up the iPad and then install the update.

REMEMBER

When you restore an iPad, your passwords aren't restored with the other data. You'll need to re-enter all your passwords, such as those used by the Apple Store, your e-mail accounts, VPN settings, websites, and your apps.

You should always back up your iPad before installing an iOS update so, if something goes wrong, all your data and settings are preserved. When updating iOS, you should plug the iPad in to a power source, to avoid the battery running out of juice in the middle of the upgrade, which can require you to wipe out and restore the iPad.

Tried-and-True Troubleshooting

Your iPad may appear to be a model of efficiency and reliability, but sometimes it just doesn't work as it should. Try the techniques in this feature to straighten out any such bad behavior.

Restarting your iPad

To restart your iPad, press and hold the Sleep/Wake button until the Slide to Power Off arrow appears at the top of the screen; then slide that arrow to the right. This action turns off your iPad. Wait a few seconds and then press the Sleep/Wake button to turn the iPad back on.

If the Slide to Power Off arrow doesn't appear, press and hold both the Sleep/Wake and Home buttons for several seconds to force the iPad to shut down. Then wait a few seconds and press Sleep/Wake. The Apple logo appears as the iPad restarts.

Force-quitting frozen apps

Sometimes an iPad app freezes, and pressing Home to switch to another app doesn't work. If that happens, the iPad has an easy technique to force that app to quit: Press and hold the Home button for six to ten seconds. If that doesn't work, force your iPad to restart.

Problems with networks

If you're having problems with Wi-Fi or your cellular carrier's network (if you have a Wi-Fi/cellular model), try these techniques before seeking professional help:

Wi-Fi (top) and cellular (bottom) signal strength from best (left) to worst (right)

- ✔ **Make sure Wi-Fi and/or cellular data are turned on.** Maybe you put the iPad in Airplane mode and forgot to turn that off, for example. Go to the Settings app, make sure Airplane Mode is set to Off in the Sidebar. Make sure Wi-Fi is turned on (tap Wi-Fi in the Sidebar to get the Wi-Fi controls). Make sure cellular data is turned on (if you have a cellular iPad with an active cellular data plan) by tapping Cellular Data in the Sidebar and then making sure the Cellular Data switch is set to On in the Cellular Data pane that appears. If you have a third-gen iPad, remember that you can turn off the 4G LTE feature in the same pane; LTE is faster but uses more battery power, so if you needed to stretch your battery life, you might have turned off LTE temporarily and forgot to turn it back on.

- ✔ **Make sure you have sufficient Wi-Fi or cellular signal strength.** Check the status bar to see whether the number of arcs displayed for Wi-Fi signal strength or the number of bars for cellular is at least two. Try moving around to get a better signal — metal, stone, concrete, and other dense objects can block even nearby signals. If you're using Wi-Fi, make sure you're using an available network with the strongest signal; your iPad may have stuck with a network you used earlier, even though a stronger one is now available. (Tap Wi-Fi in the Sidebar of the Settings app to see available Wi-Fi networks and switch to a new one.)

- ✔ **Restart your iPad.** This can clear up errors in the iPad's memory or force it to abandon network settings that it should have updated but didn't (such as when you moved from one Wi-Fi access point to another).

Apple offers two very good articles that may help you with Wi-Fi issues. The first (available at **http://support.apple.com/kb/TS3237**) offers some general troubleshooting tips and hints; the second (available at **http://support.apple.com/kb/HT1365**) explains potential sources of interference for wireless devices and networks.

If none of the preceding suggestions fixes your network issues, try resetting your iPad.

Resetting your iPad

Little kids playing sports often end an argument by agreeing to a do-over. The iPad has its own do-over capability: The Reset settings. You use these for either of two purposes: To erase information on an iPad you're giving to someone else, so it is cleaned of your preferences and data; or to try to fix an ill-behaved iPad by erasing settings that may have gotten corrupted in the iPad's memory.

You find the reset options in the Settings app. Tap General in the Sidebar and then tap Reset at the bottom of the General pane that appears.

- **Reset All Settings:** Resets all settings, but no data or media is deleted. This might fix an ill-behaved iPad.

- **Erase All Content and Settings:** Resets all settings *and* wipes out all your data. Use this option before giving your iPad permanently to someone else.

- **Reset Network Settings:** Deletes the current network settings and restores them to their factory defaults. This might help network access issues.

- **Subscriber Services:** Deletes the carrier information for a cellular-enabled iPad and requires you to re-register your iPad to get service.

- **Reset Keyboard Dictionary:** Removes added words from the dictionary, so use it if your dictionary has gotten full of incorrect corrections.

REMEMBER

The iPad keyboard is intelligent. And, one reason it's so smart is that it learns from you. So when you reject words that the iPad keyboard suggests, it figures that the words you specifically banged out ought to be added to the keyboard dictionary.

- **Reset Home Screen Layout:** Reverts all icons to the way they were at the factory. There's little use for this control.

- **Reset Location Warnings:** Restores factory defaults. Use this to get confirmation notices for apps and services that want to use your location information — even those you previously gave permission to.

Restoring your iPad

The most drastic action you can take to reset your iPad is to restore it. Restoring an iPad wipes out its settings and data — returning the device to its factory condition — and then reinstalls from iTunes on your computer all the applications and data backed up there for your iPad.

Fortunately, backing up is part of syncing, so when you sync your iPad, you're also backing it up. Sync often so you don't get sunk. To restore an iPad, connect it to your computer via a USB cable. Then launch iTunes. Select your iPad in the Sidebar's Devices list and go to the Summary pane. Click Restore and follow the instructions. Note that if you use iCloud backup, those settings are restored when you log into your iCloud account, as are any media purchased at the iTunes Store, but any other data is lost unless you restore from your computer's backup.

Restore: Drastic but sometimes necessary

More help on the Apple website

If you try everything suggested in this feature and still have problems with your iPad, you can check out some other places before you throw in the towel and smash the iPad into tiny little pieces (or ship it back to Apple for repairs):

- **Apple offers an excellent set of support resources on its website:** Go to **www.apple.com/support/ipad/getstarted**. There, you can browse support issues by category, search for a problem by keyword, read or download technical manuals, and scan the discussion forums.

- **Apple has tons of discussion forums about almost every aspect of using your iPad:** Go directly to them at **http://discussions.apple.com**. They're chock-full of useful questions and answers from other iPad users, and we find that if you can't get an answer to a question elsewhere, you can often find it in these forums. You can browse by category (Syncing, for example) or search by keyword.

DUMMIES